MW00441235

MY MADONNA
A Memoir by Norris W. Burroughs

Copyright © 2012 by Norris W. Burroughs
All rights reserved.

Published in the United States by
Whimsy Literary Agency LLC

Book and cover design: www.MeyerNewYork.com
cover photograph © Inga Ivanova/Bigstock.com

ISBN-10: 0988413604
ISBN-13: 978-0-9884136-0-3

10 9 8 7 6 5 4 3 2 1
First Edition

ACKNOWLEDGEMENTS

To my family for their support
and to
Steve Brower, for knowing who I am.

MY MADONNA
MY INTIMATE FRIENDSHIP WITH THE BLUE EYED GIRL
ON HER ARRIVAL IN NEW YORK

A MEMOIR BY

NORRIS W. BURROUGHS

WHIMSY LITERARY AGENCY, LLC
NEW YORK

"Burroughs was ideally placed to bring to life a pivotal era in music history. *My Madonna* is a touching, nuanced account of his fortuitous relationship with a legendary performer."

MY MADONNA

TABLE OF CONTENTS

INTRODUCTION

For as long as I can remember, I have believed in the existence of spirits. In using this word, I don't necessarily mean anything supernatural, although that is not entirely out of the question. When I speak of spirits, I am usually referring to spirited human beings. Much of our lives generally seem prosaic, a series of routine events that we are compelled to repeat from birth to death. Sometimes, during the course of our lives, we encounter beings that seem to be unshackled by this wheel of repetition. In my life, I have been fortunate to know more than my share of such creatures. As an artist and someone who has moved in artistic circles, I've encountered people who have a spark of magnetic energy, a charisma that sets them apart from the general population. Madonna is one such spirit.

What is more, I witnessed at first hand Madonna's ascent to prominence, a journey that was dizzying in its speed and totality. I saw the final result of the exercise of human will and ambition, combined with a sense of timing and instinct that bordered on the supernatural.

The strangeness of my encounter is that having been intimate with her, it is difficult for me to reconcile my memory with the person she has become. When I first met Madonna, she had barely been in New York for three months. Having lived there for so many years of my life, it is easy for me to forget how many people come from all corners of the globe to the Emerald City in pursuit of a dream.

Even for a native, this town has the capacity to surprise with its wild manifestations of exuberance. It is both heaven and hell for aspiring actors, dancers, artists and musicians. Upon her arrival in New York, Madonna's ascent began almost immediately, and I became not only her friend and lover, but also a part of the chain of events that led directly to the fulfillment of her dream.

I take no credit for Madonna's success. Had I not introduced her to Dan Gilroy, I'm quite certain that she would have eventually found her way to a career as a pop star by some other route. The best that I can say about my contributions is that in a strange way, I embodied the frenetic and eclectic energy of New York City. I was someone who was plugged in to the mainline, with one foot in the underground and the other in high culture. In essence that is what New York represents to me. It is a place where the twain shall meet and do so regularly. I've always instinctively understood that, and that's why Madonna chose me. –NB

CHAPTER ONE
THE LEOPARD GIRL 1978

The girl in the leopard skin tights whirled around the room like a dervish. She was dancing to the *Village People's* hit song "YMCA". She leaped and spun, her wild brown mane flying, possessed by the spirit of exhibitionism. The other dancers on the floor, aware that a new breed of mutant was in their midst, egged her on: "All right, Ma-Donna!"

It was the late fall of 1978, and I was making the scene at a party in the Upper West Side home of choreographer Pearl Lang, a former Martha Graham star, and her husband Joseph Wiseman, a character actor who played James Bond's nemesis, Dr. No. I had arrived with my buddy Michael, a dancer studying with Lang.

It was a wild Saturday night, with a bunch of modern dancers getting disco funky in the spacious living room, and the leopard girl was setting the pace. Mike and I leaped like the drunken fools we were onto the dance floor, bellowing out the song's lyrics: "*That's when someone came up to me and said, Young Man, you can live in a tree... On your knees...*" Whatever! We were gone! Out of our minds! The leopard girl's energy was holding us in thrall. She was in her element, center stage. As she whirled around, her movements took on the quality of a ritual, as if she was dancing in a ring of fire. As I danced, I casually moved closer to her on the floor, but she whirled away from me, seemingly unaware of my interest in her.

I stepped away momentarily to watch her, to study the intricacy of her moves. There was something decidedly feline and predatory in the way that she was dancing. She would spin deliriously and then suddenly crouch as if to gather herself.

Then she would leap high in the classical ballet move known as Grand jeté, where the dancer does a mid-air split. She would suddenly land like a cat on all fours and stretch out. It was one of the most subtly sexual things I'd ever seen, without being overt. The sexuality was in her essence, and didn't require much in the way of clichéd embellishments to augment it.

During a quieter moment, I sidled up to her in the kitchen to introduce myself. She was leaning against the refrigerator, drinking orange juice. She was wearing a pale turquoise pullover with a low neckline and the sleeves pushed up to her elbows, with those impossible orange leopard print tights. Her body was lean and muscular but still curvaceous and feminine, with the proportions of a renaissance statue. Her skin was pale and luminous, and the contrast between its tone and her dark wavy hair and blue-green eyes was striking.

There was something about the way she stood, poised, yet casual that got to me. There was a subtle air of defiance, which felt like a challenge. As she turned to watch my approach, there was also a flash of recognition that passed between our eyes. One sensualist can always recognize another.

Someone passed a joint to her. She took one toke and handed it to me, smiling sweetly.

"Thanks," I said. I took the obligatory hit and passed it on. "I'm Norris."

"Madonna!" she replied coyly, flashing her large eyes at me. A young brown-skinned man standing next to her cut in. "You mean like Lady Madonna?"

"Get lost!" she said scornfully. "I hate that shit! Every idiot says that!"

She turned back to me. "Do you have anything original to say?" I was taken aback, challenged by her directness. Here was a woman who did not suffer fools gladly. It was an enormous turn-on and I felt compelled to rise to the occasion.

"I love the way you dance," I said. "Have you been studying with Pearl for very long?"

"No, I've only been in New York for a few months. I studied back home in Michigan. It's great here. I feel like I totally belong."

Madonna reached over with her forefinger and stroked my bicep. A charge of electricity went through me.

"Nice arms. You look like Marlon Brando in *A Streetcar Named Desire*. Are you a dancer?"

"No, I came here with my friend Michael."

"He's a good dancer. He's really strong. I've partnered with him and he can lift me over his head."

"Yeah, he's a great Adagio dancer. He's really acrobatic. Did you study Ballet as well?"

"Oh Yeah, since I was twelve. Listen, I've got to go talk to Pearl. I'll see you later."

I felt as if she had suddenly cut me off. It was something that I would become used to, being dismissed in that curt fashion that she had.

I caught sight of her later on in the living room, a social butterfly surrounded by her potential suitors. I didn't feel up to the challenge of competing for her attention. I saw her dancing with Michael. They were doing a sort of prancing step, which as a non-dancer, I was reluctant to try to imitate. Lang's style was modern, but all the dancers, including Madonna seemed firmly grounded in classical ballet technique. I was beginning to feel out of my element, so I decided to take my leave.

Something told me that I would see her again.

Sunday morning I got a phone call. "Hi, it's Madonna. I'm over at Michael's place. So, why don't you get your gorgeous Brando body over here?"

Michael had spent a chaste night with her. He had been going steady with another girl and he was feeling guilty about his potential infidelity. Madonna was getting bored with his guilty conscience. She had brazenly asked him for my phone number and Michael had seen a way out of his dilemma. I suggested that they both come over for brunch at my place, which was on 61st Street and 1st Avenue.

She was wearing someone's cast off clothing - loose fitting brown corduroy trousers and a nubbly wool turtleneck sweater - looking like an angelic, dead end kid, with her thumb poking through a hole in her sleeve. The three of us sat around chatting and drinking coffee. After about a half hour, I noticed that Madonna was focusing the lion's share of her attention on me, and I of course could not take my eyes off her. Michael quickly picked up on his cue and took off, as he had planned to do.

I put Stevie Wonder's *Songs in the Key of Life* on the turntable and Madonna and I both sang along enthusiastically to the song "Knocks Me Off My Feet."

"You have a beautiful voice," I said.

"So do you," she replied.

"This is Stevie's best album," I said. "You must love *Motown* coming from so close to Detroit."

"Oh, Yeah. That's the first music I can remember that really made me dance. *The Supremes...* The *Jacksons*. I couldn't sit still."

She removed her heavy sweater in the warmth of the room to reveal a black danskin tank top.

As the sun shone through the window on her pale skin and mass of light brown curls, I found myself transported. I had the eerie sense that I had known her once long ago in another lifetime. It was my affinity with the Italian Renaissance that was triggering the illusion, but it was an overwhelming sensation of déjà vu.

"Do you know that your face is exactly the same as a painting of the Madonna by Botticelli?"

"Really, I'll have to see that sometime," she said enthusiastically.

I asked her to tell me a bit about herself. She stared thoughtfully into her coffee mug.

"I really just got to New York this summer, from Michigan.

I didn't know anyone here, but I knew I wanted to come to New York and be a dancer, so here I am. Christopher Flynn, my ballet teacher encouraged me to come here. He was a sadistic bastard, but I love him to death. He used to hit us with a stick."

"He did what?"

"He did worse than that. He had a wicked tongue on him too. I hung out with him. He took me to galleries… museums… He was gay and he took me to all the wild clubs in Detroit. We'd get out on the dance floor and they'd make room for us. He whipped my ass into shape. I could never have dared audition for Pearl if he hadn't psyched me up."

"Pearl's stuff is pretty wild!" I said.

"I love her style," Madonna said." It's so angst ridden."

It was an apt description of the somewhat tormented quality of Lang's work.

"Where do you live?" I asked.

"I'm living uptown, in Morningside Heights with a guy who's going to Columbia University. He's not my boyfriend, or anything."

"Are you seeing anyone?" I asked.

"No one steady. I spend a lot of time practicing and almost all the men I'm with are gay. You know dancers."

"Yeah, Michael tells me that he gets shit from them about being straight. It's like there's some sort of gay mafia in the dance world."

She laughed. " That's a good one. I'll have to use that some time."

I tried to place her accent. It kept shifting, sometimes sounding cultured, almost British, other times languidly Southern. She certainly didn't sound like a Midwesterner. It occurred to me that she was, like me, someone who had unconsciously absorbed aspects of different people and things that had attracted her. Already drawn to her physically, I was falling in love with her mind as well. She seemed suddenly softer and less edgy, as if she was relaxing and letting down her guard.

"How did you get the name Madonna?" I asked her.

"It was my mother's name. She was French Canadian."

"But your last name, Ciccone is Italian, right?"

"Oh yeah. My father's old school Italian. My grandparents came from Pacentro, near Rome. Some of the popes used to vacation there, so the people are really devout. My Dad's favorite expression was, 'If it feels good, then you're doing something wrong.'" Madonna was suddenly curious about my guitar sitting in its case in the corner.

"Do you play much?" she asked

"I'm in a band."

"Really? Play me something."

I took out my Gibson SG and without plugging it in I played an old Elvis tune, "One Night With You."

"Very cool," she said, after I'd finished. "I love Elvis. You do a nice impression of him. Similar, but still like it's your own thing. Did you know that he died on my birthday? I've felt connected to him ever since."

She reached over and stroked the instrument's neck. "Can I see the guitar?"

I handed it to her and she moved from the chair to the edge of the bed to give herself more room. She strummed absently.

"I used to play the piano when I was a kid," she said. "I hated the lessons but I've always wanted to play music."

"Well, why don't you?" I said.

"Maybe I will."

She gazed at me, her eyes suddenly brighter.

"What I like about you is that you have dark hair and blue eyes like me."

I moved in closer, reaching out and grasping her hand. She took mine and touched it to her lips. Then she reached over and touched mine.

"I like your mouth too," she said. "I'll bet it fits really well with mine." I leaned over and kissed her softly, then harder, our lips blending, lingering. I gently pushed her backwards onto the bed and began stroking her chest. She pulled me closer and rolled on top of me, grinding slowly. As she kissed me more hungrily, I could see how much she enjoyed the play of our lips together. It was more than simply foreplay, but a complete sexual act unto itself.

She ran her tongue around the inside of my mouth and then across my lips. Then she moved down the side of my neck and inside my clavicle.

"Mmmm! You taste nice and salty sweet." She teased me, sending shivers down my spine. The signals that I was receiving from her said that she wanted me right then and there. I was confident, "young, dumb and full of come" and used to having my way with women fairly quickly. I slipped the strap of her tank top down her shoulder and exposed her breast. I began stroking it gently causing her to moan softly. She kissed my mouth again hungrily. After what seemed a long time, she pulled away abruptly.

"Listen, I've got to go."

"I'm sorry!" I said. "Perhaps I was going too fast."

"No. It's fine. You really turn me on, but I have an appointment to keep."

I was again struck with the suddenness of her departure. It had felt as if we had been in some sort of zone, comfortably getting to know each other, and suddenly she was off. This was the second time that I saw the restlessness she has become famous for.

Legend has it that Madonna Louise Veronica Ciccone arrived in New York City on a sweltering August day, wearing a winter coat and carrying one suitcase. The story goes that she quickly found lodgings from a stranger who approached her. Regardless of the truth of varying accounts of her arrival, Madonna's purpose was crystal clear. She was determined to study with Pearl Lang, whose avant-garde modern dance style appealed strongly to her. This wild and impulsive leap into the unknown put Madonna on the fast track into a strange world that had more often than not consumed those whose dreams drew them into it.

Madonna would be one the few people whose vision and will power was up to the challenge of the Empire City. Regardless of the obstacle, her wiles, instincts and raw talent would always find a way to overcome.

The city that Madonna had recently arrived in was in a frozen chrysalis state, waiting to be renewed. It had only been two years since President Gerald Ford had told New York City to drop dead and it seemed that the town was doing a pretty good job of doing just that.

In 1977 the city had been plagued by a brutal and demented killer known as "Son of Sam," who executed his victims with a 44-caliber pistol, sending shockwaves of fear throughout the five Boroughs. That same summer, during a sweltering heat wave a massive blackout brought the city to standstill for several days.

On the verge of bankruptcy, it felt like Dodge City in more ways than one. The infrastructure of the bustling metropolis was in serious disrepair and buildings and subway trains were covered with graffiti.

Growing up in New York, I had always been aware of the rotten apple quality that the city was partially famous for. It was actually part of the charm of the city. It seemed that all sorts of people of varying socio-economic backgrounds and lifestyles were living around the corner from each other, particularly in the east and west sides of Greenwich Village, which was popular for starving artists and people who craved the Bohemian flavor. Still, the mid- to late 70s was a come down for most residents after the economic high points of the late 50s and 60s. A heroin epidemic on the Lower East Side, Upper West Side and the outer boroughs, particularly the Bronx, was a devastating plague that bred crime and dissolution.

This was my town, a city that I had explored from top to bottom. Born in East Harlem, I had moved to the North Bronx with my family when I was five. As soon as I was old enough, I had ridden my bicycle across the bridge at 207th Street into Manhattan to explore. At 13, I had ridden all the way downtown, from upper Broadway to 110th Street and Central Park, then down from Columbus Circle, through Times Square and down 6th Avenue to Greenwich Village and finally all the way to Battery Park. Then I had taken the long subway ride back uptown to my relatively placid Bronx neighborhood.

By the late 60s even my area, on the east side of Bronx Park began to change. The South Bronx had always seemed a hellhole, but by the early 1970s, that neighborhood was literally on fire and the rot seemed to be creeping further and further north.

There were some compensations for the decay. As usual, the most vibrant scene was downtown, in clubs that catered to hard-edged punk music. Those that aspired to the mantle of punk took pride in the grungy danger of the mean streets and the dimly lit clubs that stank of beer and stale piss.

The forerunner in the early seventies had been *Max's Kansas City*, a somewhat upscale looking bar on 18th Street and Park Avenue that was home to the edgy *New York Dolls*. The *Dolls* had pioneered a style of dress and music that took no prisoners. The band was raw and unpretentious and outfitted themselves in a combination of street-tough rags and transvestite drag. A few years later, British entrepreneur, Malcolm McLaren would bring the *Dolls* to England and try to jump-start their career. Failing to do so, McLaren would then create what he envisioned as his own version of the *Dolls*, the *Sex Pistols*, thereby kicking off the UK punk movement.

Inherent in the *Dolls* and early punk in general was the unique flavor of the New York City streets: New York had a vibrant street life unlike any other. In the early to mid-1960s, Max's had become a hangout for Andy Warhol's minions, a motley crew of drag queens, greasers, rock n' rollers, low rent actors and bohemian artists.

I became a regular at Max's in 1972, when my friend Lynn had taken me there. Lynn was outspoken and loved meeting colorful new people. She quickly introduced me to several in the Warhol crowd, notably one Eric Emerson, the Magic Tramp. Eric was infamous for showing his prodigious cock in and out of Warhol films such as *Heat* in which he is constantly jacking off. Several years earlier, Emerson had been given the responsibility of squiring rock god Jim Morrison around the scene, scoring groupies for him and keeping him from getting arrested. The club was a magnet for those seeking the new and the strange in the big city. *Led Zeppelin* would show up to hang out when in town, shock rocker *Alice Cooper* was a regular and David Bowie was an occasional visitor.

In and out of a half dozen garage bands, I found myself a fly on the wall in the bar's dark back room, witnessing all sorts of bizarre activity. The back room was a theatrical event, where the regulars would often prepare themselves prior to their entrance. The lighting was distinctive, a dim lurid red.

There was a strong sense of hierarchy there, and if you didn't belong or at least look good, you might feel the scorn of those who were the chosen ones. Upstairs was the cabaret, a small room with an even smaller stage that had seen many a band come and go. The lovely Bebe Buell-queen of the groupies-was a regular at Max's and would scout out the dressing room on the upstairs landing, looking for her next conquest.

One night upstairs, Eric Emerson introduced Lynn and me to proto-punk singer, Iggy Pop who was doing a series of shows at Max's. Eric and Iggy, both long- haired blondes, were dressed in identical gold lamé jock straps. Bebe had quickly moved in on Iggy, admiring his sleek, naked, muscular torso.

On stage that night, Iggy Pop leaped onto a table and fell

to the floor on a bell glass, slashing his upper abdomen and spraying the room with blood. Iggy would have carried on singing, had he not been forcibly rushed from the room and to the hospital. A few nights later, he was back, sporting a neat row of sutures on his bare sternum.

Gradually, the scene shifted to a club on the Bowery, called *CBGB*, where groups like *The Ramones, Blondie, Patty Smith, the Talking Heads* and *Television* built their reputations by defining the sound that would become punk music. Punk was essentially the New York street rocker's response to what they perceived as the excess of arena rock bands such as *Led Zeppelin* and *The Who*, art rock bands like *Yes* and *Genesis* and the sickly lush over-production of disco music, which seemed to be more about the arrangement than anything else.

On the other hand, disco was thriving in the arena of *Studio 54* and clubs like it. Although the mainstream was gradually moving away from disco as a phenomenon, club dance music would remain viable, particularly in the Black and Gay communities. DJs like Frankie Knuckles and Larry Levan would eventually create a powerful underground style from disco that would come to be known as House music.

In 1979, the punk group *Blondie*, fronted by chanteuse Deborah Harry, released a track called "Heart of Glass", which scandalized the punk world by having the temerity to have a disco beat. It was deemed a massive betrayal by many of the punk faithful, but it was a huge hit record. Up until the advent of *Blondie*, female rockers were few and far between, but the band's vocalist, Deborah Harry, a former Max's barmaid, would make a huge impression on women like Madonna, empowering them to step forward.

Several years away from the gentrification of the 1980s, it was still possible to find cheap places to live, and artists and musicians took over huge loft spaces in the lower Manhattan neighborhoods of Soho and Tribeca. Up in the South Bronx, poverty and a rampant drug culture saw the growth of street gangs, which would enable musicians such as Afrika Bambaataa to spread hip-hop culture with his Zulu Nation movement. NewYork City was a wild jungle-a jumble of roiling, simmering elements that refused to melt but shifted and morphed into new and vital forms. The music being born would nurture Madonna's lust for experimentation with herself and her style. Although she had come to New York to study dance, the rush she was getting from Pearl Lang's company was merely Madonna's gateway drug. Soon, she would be hooked on the real juice, the energy that made the town the entertainment capital of the world.

CHAPTER TWO
RIVERSIDE PARK

A few days later, I visited Madonna in Morningside Heights. She was living in a small room in a large apartment, uptown near Riverside Park. This is one of the most spectacular neighborhoods in New York City. The hills of the park run down to the Hudson River, which makes its stately way north to upstate New York. Riverside Drive, running alongside, features some of the grandest classical and Gothic architecture you are likely to see anywhere. This was a neighborhood that Madonna, with her Renaissance Botticelli face, seemed to belong in. The apartment had five or six rooms and a long narrow hallway. Madonna's room was sparsely furnished, with a mattress on the floor and little else. It felt like a medieval monk's cell. As someone who had recently arrived in town, it made sense that Madonna had few possessions with which to adorn her space. Still, I had a strong feeling that she wouldn't be staying there for very long.

It was a lovely warm late afternoon for mid November, and I suggested we go for a walk in the park. We ambled slowly down a path towards the river as the sun began to set, and sat under a tree on a grassy knoll. Down the slope was the embankment of the river, nearly a mile wide, with the Palisades of New Jersey on the other side. I could feel the pulsing energy of the water, as heavy as the blood pumping through me.

"I can't stay at Rob's place too much longer," she said. "He keeps coming on to me. If I don't put out, he'll put me out!"

"Well, as you can see, I don't have a lot of space, but you can stay with me, at least for a while," I offered.

'I'll think about it. I think I may have a place lined up

nearby, but it's with a bunch of people."

I moved closer to her, my lips brushing the nape of her neck. Our eyes met, dreamily. Her eyes were a mystical deep liquid blue green with unusually long lashes. They were feline, dangerous and bewitching. My mouth devoured hers and we fell onto the grass in a long embrace as she twisted her suppleness around me. As I caressed her, time seemed to stand still and I wished that it would do so in reality. I could feel Madonna letting go the more we spent time together. I could no longer sense restlessness in every fiber of her body. She seemed content just to lie there in my arms in the gathering darkness.

After the sunset, we walked slowly back up the embankment, towards Riverside Church. We stood staring up at the stars that swirled above the towering church spire. It did not feel like we were in America, but in some timeless otherworldly European dreamscape. We entered the church and gazed at the opulence of its huge stained glass windows.

"This church was modeled after Chartres Cathedral in France, you know," I said.

"It's fabulous!" she replied. "I've always loved churches. My dad was a really devout Catholic."

"Did you go to parochial school?"

"Yeah, I had this thing about nuns. I thought that being a nun was the coolest thing in the world, since they got to be the brides of Christ."

In that moment, it occurred to me that the iconic significance of Madonna's name would have been a factor in her emotional development and in her attitude towards the church. Growing up with that name must have felt like both a blessing and a curse to her. Of course I could have had no idea of what was to come, but the notion aroused a peculiar sense of premonition in me. Her name and personality seemed larger than life and fraught with destiny. When she became famous, it appeared that Madonna had a compulsion to exploit the imagery of Catholicism, to the point of what some critics considered desecration. In the video of her song "*Like a Prayer*" Madonna shocked conventions by using images of burning crosses and of her own bleeding stigmata to convey her passionate message.

Her lifelong fascination and conflicted feelings towards the ritual and symbols of Christianity revealed a desire to test the boundaries that her upbringing had imposed.

We left the church and walked leisurely over to Broadway for ice cream cones. Madonna asked for extra sprinkles, indulging an obvious sweet tooth. After strolling on Broadway for a few minutes, I took her back to her room. We stood outside in the hallway for several minutes, kissing softly. I asked her if I could come inside.

"I've got to get up really early for class tomorrow," she said. "We're working on a piece that's really strenuous. Listen, I'd really love to spend the rest of the night kissing you."

She punctuated the statement with another long kiss.

After a final embrace Madonna pulled away. She went inside, and still looking coyly over her shoulder she slowly closed the door.

Later on that evening, I thought about her. She seemed to be the hungriest person I had ever known. Certain people can trip a switch in the brain that allows you to see their whole potential, to see what they will become, like a hologram, any part of which contains information about the whole. Seeing Madonna was like seeing her whole life taking place simultaneously, rather than in sequential space and time. I barely knew her, and yet I was strangely aware that she was marked, chosen for a life in a stratosphere so rare that few will ever know its like.

There was something inside her, a force so powerful that could not be sated by ordinary living. She tried to cover up her yearning with a devil-may-care streetwise façade, but it would continue to emerge at strange intervals. She would become restless, as if things were not moving quickly enough for her ambition. Sometimes she was sweet and vulnerable, her heart open and loving, but then she would suddenly close herself off, as if to say, "Don't ask for too much. Don't get too close to me. I'm going places and you can't come along."

At that moment, I had no idea just how far away those places were and how far they would take her from me.

CHAPTER THREE
CORONA

The next day I took the subway out to Corona, in the outer borough of Queens, to visit my friend Dan and his brother Ed Gilroy. The brothers rented a building which had been a synagogue, that was a stone's throw from Flushing Meadow Park, former site of the New York World's Fair. The Gog was a large two-story structure with a nave that was perfect for a rehearsal space. Dan and Ed had a band called *The Breakfast Club*, which reminded me somewhat of a new wave version of *The Kinks*. Dan and Ed wrote basic three-chord rock n' roll with clever lyrical twists. That afternoon they were playing a quirky progression called "Eggy Ann", which featured the lyric, "*If you don't treat me right, I'm gonna put you in the frying pan*" Dan was six-foot-two and blonde, with piercing blue eyes and a handsome Irish face. He favored porkpie hats and saw himself as a cross between James Cagney and Art Carney. Eddie was about five-foot-eleven, with darker hair and sharper features. Both brothers radiated intelligence and strong senses of humor.

The Breakfast Club had been trying to score a gig at *CBGB*, but when they called the club to inquire about an audition, they were repeatedly told that the owner, Hilly Kristal, "Can't come to the phone right now." I was playing in a band named *Steel Breeze*, and we had also sent a tape to *CBGB*. The general feeling was that we just were not punk enough for that scene. Dan, Ed and I decided that we needed to find other venues where we could perform, perhaps together.

Dan and I also worked together as textile designers in the garment center. Both of us were artists who had been hoodwinked into the shmatte trade because we had started out in a hand-painted T-shirt company in the mid seventies. We had first met in the artist's loft of the T-shirt Company called *The Lotus Shop* on St. Marks Place in the East Village. Dan and I had an immediate rapport because of the similar nature of our senses of humor and our mutual attraction to art and music. As is often the case with two strong willed friends, there was a measure of rivalry between us. We both recognized the similarity of our drives to excel, and often tried to outdo the other. We also shared a similar taste in women, and would often date the same girls at the same time. This was a pattern that would soon manifest again with memorable results.

The Lotus Shop gradually shifted its focus from T-shirts to hand-painted high fashion garments, changing its name to *Gossamer Wing*. The Wing, as we called it, was run by design director Barbara Leach, who had a strong eye for color. Barbara was a natural diplomat, who had a way of mollifying and stroking the egos of temperamental artists as well as clients.

Another of our co-workers was a brilliant gay theatrical costume designer named Bernard Roth, who often worked for off-Broadway director, John Vaccaro. The driving force behind the revolutionary *"Playhouse of the Ridiculous,"* Vaccaro pioneered the use of gay camp themes and highly surrealistic sets and costumes in avant-garde theater. Bernard worked hard with us during the day and in the evenings he worked for the Playhouse. In the wee hours of the morning he would often join the fast track gay party crowd, burning the candle at both ends.

Bernard had named the textile company *Gossamer Wing*, after the lyric from a Cole Porter song. We were fortunate to acquire couture designer Mary McFadden as our main client, in order to create masterpieces of China silk batik for her. It was an okay way to make a living, but it was not natural for me. I had little or no affinity for fashion and it felt as if I was merely spinning my wheels. However, I was making friends and associates there, many of whom I would keep in close contact with over the years. Although my job at the Wing would do little to further my own artistic ambitions, it would be useful to Madonna in the long run.

I had a second job as well. On Saturdays, I would work at a store on 64thStreet and Lexington called *The T-Shirt Gallery*. I was the custom T-shirt artist, hand-painting designs per customer request. My flier posted in the window stated that I would paint whatever fantasy scenario you desired. As a result, I ended up painting some strange and amusing designs for scores of people. For Sylvester Stallone, I painted a well-shredded black shirt with the words *Wild Cat* emblazoned on it. For Carrie Fisher I did a *Star Wars* motif, and I painted mythological menageries for Dustin Hoffman's children. I did a design for *Penthouse* editor Bob Guccione's girlfriend that had her racing through the night sky pulled along by several of her Rhodesian Ridgeback dogs. *The T-Shirt Gallery's* owner, who called himself Finn, had worked extensively marketing Andy Warhol's designs, a fact that he never tired of mentioning.

One afternoon I was doing a custom airbrush design of an angel. I was laying out a voluptuous winged creature on a large T-shirt when Madonna stopped by the store to visit me.

"What are you drawing?" she asked.

"It's a custom angel."

'I'm an angel. I'll pose for it."

And she sat for twenty minutes while I modeled a very Renaissance flavored angel after her classical pose. I could see that Madonna was quite adept at posing. Like most dancers, she had a keen awareness of how the subtlest shift in her body could alter the nuance of the pose.

I now realize that I have always had a thing for dancers, perhaps since I was ten years old and saw the film *West Side Story* and its wild, unorthodox combination of ballet, modern and Latin dance. Coming out of the theater after seeing that film, I found myself doing grand jeté leaps down Allerton Avenue. Then I noticed that I wasn't alone in this ridiculous exuberance, since half the neighborhood kids were leaping about like kangaroos.

One of my first girlfriends was Claudia Brown, who studied dance at the *New York School of Ballet* on the Upper West side. The school's owners were Barbara and Richard Thomas, parents of John-Boy Walton actor Richard Thomas. Elliot Feld, who played Baby John in *West Side Story*, was also a student. Strangely, although Feld was one of the most accomplished dancers to appear in the film, he never got to dance much in it.

I spent a good deal of time hanging around Claudia's school watching her rehearse, and even took a class or two, but I was totally inept. Claudia would eventually appear in *Saturday Night Fever*, as the stunning girl in the red dress who danced with Travolta.

Several days later, Madonna called in the evening, wanting to come visit me. When she arrived, she seemed anxious. She began to complain about how strenuous her dance classes were.

"I hurt my back in class today! I don't think that I'm eating enough quality protein. I'm a vegetarian, you know, and I can't afford to eat well. I'm just not healing fast enough!"

"Yeah, dancing is rough," I replied. "Dancers always seem to have injuries."

"That's what Pearl said when I complained. She said to get used to it. It goes with the territory."

I had gone shopping earlier, and my refrigerator was full of food.

"Let me cook you some tofu with veggies and brown rice," I offered. I put the rice to boil, and diced some broccoli, stirring it with sautéed mushrooms and onions in a wok. I added the tofu last with a little soy sauce and poured Madonna a glass of white wine. "Take it easy," I said as I handed her a plate.

After dinner, I started to massage the muscles of her

upper back. She was lean, but her rhomboid and trapezius muscles were thick and powerful. Her back was a thing of extraordinary beauty, as when god or nature creates something that is perfectly functional yet exquisitely symmetrical. My massage strokes followed her spinal erector muscles as they flowed seamlessly into a gorgeous tight round ass. She sighed with pleasure. "Please don't stop. That is the absolute best." After a few minutes, my hands began to stray, gently tracing the shape of her ribs and upward to her breasts. I kissed the back of her neck and then moved to her eager lips. She put her arms around my neck and I gently lifted her onto the bed. We moved fluidly as if we were dancing, responding to the subtlest cue from the other's body. Our lovemaking was slow and sensual, with lingering caresses, as if we were trying to make a delicious meal last forever.

It was the one time that Madonna surrendered herself to me completely and I opened myself to her perhaps as much as I have ever done. It is a night I will long remember fondly.

We fell asleep around midnight, and I awoke at 2:00 a.m. with the moon shining through the window. Madonna was sitting in a chair, staring out onto 1st Avenue, lost in thought. She turned to me.

"I can't sleep. I'm a bit of an insomniac."

"Come to bed," I said. "I'll massage you back to sleep."

The following morning, the golden sunlight poured into my east-facing windows like honey. I put Ella Fitzgerald's *Cole Porter Songbook* album on the turntable, brewed strong Italian roast coffee and made us scrambled eggs for breakfast. It was a Friday, but I had the day off. We lounged about, chatting and watching T.V.

"So, do you have a steady job?" I asked her.

"I model for art classes sometimes, but I don't have much money. I'm going to have to make more soon, because I'm moving into that place on 125th Street, with three other people."

She looked over at my Spartan bookshelf.

"You have some cool books. What is that? Nureyev's biography?"

"Oh yeah. I used to see him dancing at Lincoln Center in the late sixties. Amazing. Like a fucking Centaur. He was dancing with Margot Fonteyn, and she was like fifty, but he made her look like a sixteen year old girl"

She thumbed through the book, which was full of black and white photographs of the charismatic dancer in his prime.

"This book is incredible!" she said.

"Take it. It's yours."

Madonna asked me if I had any old jeans that I no longer wanted. I tossed her a pair of Levi 501 blue jeans with a 36-inch waist that was quite large, even for me. She tried them on and they were much too big for her, but she cinched her belt tightly and wore them anyway. Most of Madonna's clothes seemed to be second hand, as she didn't have much money to spend on a wardrobe. Very little of what she wore was traditionally feminine, but her innate sense of style generally made even the most motley ensemble look compelling.

Shortly before noon, we walked west, to the Central Park Zoo. It had turned crisp and colder and Madonna was wearing an old purple coat with a fur collar.

We strolled under the big mechanical merry go round clock and headed for the Big Cat House. We stood staring at the somewhat mangy but still magnificent lion, which peered sleepily back at us.

"I'm a Leo, you know," she said. As if in response, the lion let out a mild roar and turned away.

"Really? When's your birthday?" I asked.

"I'll be 21 next August 16th."

"Wow, Napoleon's was the 15th."

"Well, he and I have a lot in common. We both want to rule the world."

"Let's go look at your friend, the leopard," I said.

The spotted cat sat perched in the crook of a scraggly tree. As we approached, it stretched, sharpening its claws on the upper branches. Madonna peered through the bars.

"I stretch like that sometimes. I feel just like that cat."

"Yeah, but you're a vegetarian," I quipped.

We continued walking west, through the park and then up Central Park West. We passed the somewhat ominous Dakota, where ex-Beatle John Lennon and conductor Leonard Bernstein lived. When we finally reached the *Museum of Natural History*, with its monumental Roman entrance strangely built over the earlier Victorian Gothic structure, we headed back east through the park. The park was spacious and inviting, even in the dim November sunlight. The paths meandered past carefully designed outcroppings of rock and artfully arranged groves of trees.

I realized in the moment how much I enjoyed walking, strolling aimlessly with Madonna. There is a carefree feeling of harmony between two people who can choose either to converse or say nothing and just enjoy the promenade. It is in these moments that the city seems to unfold magically, surrendering its secrets as one amazing locale gives way to another.

When we reached the eastern edge of the park, Madonna said, "I want to call someone that lives nearby. Her apartment just burned down, and she wants me to help her sort through some of her stuff."

Madonna picked up a pay phone and dialed. She spoke softly into the receiver. "Okay, we'll be right over." She hung up and turned to me. "We're going to the place that burned. It's just down the block. We'll have to climb up the fire escape and through the window, because the front door's blocked."

We came through the kitchen window into an apartment that had been completely gutted by fire. Madonna's friend Pam was already there, sifting through the charred rubble. "Thanks," she said to us. "You're the only ones who were willing to do this."

We spent the next hour and a half helping Pam recover what was left of her things, putting the salvageable items into cardboard boxes. When I asked what caused the fire, I got no answer. It was as if Pam didn't want to deal with the matter, so I quickly dropped the subject.

Afterwards, we walked west again to get a bite to eat, stopping at a combination restaurant-boutique called *Serendipity*. Various items of clothing ostensibly belonging to celebrities were displayed on the wall in frames. Madonna seemed fascinated by a pair of blue jeans that James Dean had supposedly died in.

I ordered a chicken sandwich, and Madonna had a banana split. Halfway through her dish, she asked the waiter for some maple syrup. She then poured a huge dollop of syrup over her desert. I gagged. "Not sweet enough for you?"

"Yum!" she said. "Listen, I've got to get to class. I'll see you soon." She kissed me sweetly and got up to leave. It had been a lovely day following an even lovelier evening. It felt like the promising early stages of a tender and loving relationship, but it was in actuality the high point before the decline.

CHAPTER FOUR
125TH STREET

A week passed and I visited Madonna in her new place. She was sharing an apartment with several roommates on west 125th street, just a half a block from the elevated train. Madonna's new room was small, but nice. The apartment was crowded, with lots of people coming and going. There was noise from the street as well as from the inhabitants, and very little privacy. It didn't feel like an ideal situation for someone as independent and opinionated as she was. Again, I didn't think that she would remain there long. It was just a few blocks from her Morningside Heights place, but the difference was vast. While the old apartment had been stately and remote, the new one was closer to Central Harlem. Up the hill towards the palisades of Riverside Park near Grant's tomb was green and inviting. Fifty yards down the hill was the rumble of the subway and the bustle of the ghetto. Madonna shut the door to her room and lay down on a mattress on the floor.

"Why don't you give me a massage?" she said.

"Are you using me for my hands?"

"Well… yes! It's just that you give great massages. You should do it for a living."

"The problem is, I only like massaging people that I like."

As I worked on the muscles of Madonna's lower back, two of her roommates came into the apartment, slamming the door loudly. It was impossible for me to concentrate.

I suggested that we go out for a bite to eat. There was no place west of her apartment, but on Broadway under the Elevated train was a small restaurant that served Cuban food and good strong espresso. We ordered coffee and flan, a caramel custard dessert and Madonna looked out of the window onto the crowded sidewalk. A lithe young Puerto Rican boy sauntered by and I saw her give him the once over.

"It's intense here," she said, "but I like it. It's full of life. I'm realizing how much I like Latin music. This isn't New York here. It's more like Nueva York. You seem to know your way around the streets pretty well here."

"Well sure. This is pretty much where I came from."

Where we sat was less than a mile from the street that I was born on. I'd lived on East 123rd street until I was five, then moved to the relative serenity and greenery of the North East Bronx. At fifteen, I returned to Harlem, near *City College* campus to attend the *High School of Music and Art*, which had an atmosphere not unlike that of the *School of Performing Arts* depicted in the movie Fame. I was more than used to youths who considered themselves superstars-to-be. One day, leaving class, my curiosity compelled me to explore the surrounding neighborhood, dangerous as it was reported to be. I'd walked down the hill from lofty Saint Nicholas Terrace, into the foreboding neighborhood streets, cutting eastward and downtown, until I stood in front of the tenement that I had spent my first five years in. I realized in that moment that during those toddler years, nearly everyone I had seen had been Black or Hispanic, with the exception of my mother. My father was a handsome, silky haired brown-skinned man, who had been a Shakespearean actor, appearing in a groundbreaking Orson Welles' all-Black production of *Macbeth*. However, standing there on that Harlem Street, I was to all intents and purposes a sixteen-year-old white boy a long ways from home, so I had better get moving before trouble found me

Few people are unaware of the significance of Harlem as the nerve center of twentieth century African-American culture. It is alternately perceived as the exotic playground of the Harlem Renaissance of the 1920's contrasted with the dangerous ghetto of the 1960's and 70's. Living on 125th

Street, Madonna, who was drawn to Black and Latin music and culture, was feeling the heat from down the hill.

At this point, however, Madonna was still focusing her attention on modern dance. Musically, she seemed to be drawn to the new wave sounds that momentarily appeared to be the hippest, most cutting edge stuff around. Disco was still big, but it was losing ground.

It was the second week of December 1978. As a band, *Steel Breeze* seemed to be losing direction or maybe just moving in a direction that I was unhappy with. My instincts were pulling towards a more Spartan sound, stripped of ostentation and virtuoso posturing. My band mates were more preoccupied with a fusion-based style relying heavily on what I felt was tedious and superfluous soloing. Guitarist Wayne and bassist Stan were excellent musicians, but behaved as if the song was merely an excuse to show off their chops. Another crucial factor working against *Steel Breeze* was that Stan and Wayne were both African American. There was a peculiar standard in rock music that stated that if you were Black, you had to play R&B. Despite the fact that Wayne's playing was reminiscent of Jimi Hendrix, it was still difficult for the suits that made the decisions as to who got signed to accept a Black rock n' roll guitarist.

I was losing interest, but I couldn't summon the momentum to move on. Occasionally, I sat in with *The Breakfast Club*, even performing a few songs at one of their shows, but it was a stylistic mismatch there as well. Playing with the Gilroy boys was fun, but seemed to hold little promise for the future.

I listened to the music that I enjoyed, but it was always an eclectic mix of genres and sounds. I went from Elvis, *The Beatles* and James Brown to Sinatra and Ella, wishing that the contemporary scene could be open to such diversity. It always seemed that a performer had a moment in which to seize the day, either by forging a new path or following the herd, and then the ride would end and the performer would become a stranded victim of the past, yearning for lost glory.

There was, of course, that occasional performer like David Bowie, who was capable of reinventing himself. Little did I realize that I was now the intimate of such a chameleon.

CHAPTER FIVE
SOHO

And so we were now dating casually but steadily. I would generally see Madonna several times a week, never asking much about whom else she was with or what she was up to the rest of the time. Since she was difficult to reach by phone, I often waited for her to call. She kept me apprised of her modeling schedule at Greene Street, an open drawing class that I could attend for a few dollars. This neighborhood is referred to as Soho, for south of Houston street, and was at that moment the artistic hub of New York. Formerly an industrial area, it had become popular with artists for its preponderance of cheap loft space. In the period from the 1950s to the 70s, scores of artists had moved downtown from Greenwich Village into spacious lofts, large single rooms of up to 3000 square feet that had been previously used by textile and other manufacturers. The architecture was singular in its use of cast iron for facades, dating from the mid 19th century, and the buildings loomed over the narrow streets in a slightly ominous way.

Initially threatening, the neighborhood would become more appealing as it was renovated and occupied, until by the 80s it would be gentrified to the degree that the artistic element was endangered and would have to relocate and pioneer another neighborhood to infuse it with Bohemian cachet.

Having done some figure modeling myself, I knew the instructors at Greene Street well, so I could sometimes recommend the poses Madonna would take. It would not be an overstatement to say that Madonna was an exhibitionist, and the posing platform was a natural spot for her. As an artist, I could appreciate the way that Madonna consciously presented herself as a living sculpture, arranging her dancer's body to its most aesthetic advantage. She was often able to strike poses that were sensually provocative without being overtly sexual. With her dance background, Madonna was capable of isolating certain segments of her anatomy in such a way that it felt as if one was seeing the human body for the first time. Although the art class is theoretically a place to express pure artistic intent, the presence of an attractive naked body is always provocative. It generally takes a good deal of concentration to ignore that aspect of the situation. Madonna obviously enjoyed the tension in the air that her nudity produced. One could say that she thrived on it.

It seemed to me that she was getting hit on a lot by horny artists, and she certainly was getting a lot of offers to pose privately. I was generally okay with this, as I knew that it went with the territory. Having dated dancers and actresses who often used their physical endowment to their advantage, I was somewhat blasé about men lusting after someone I was intimate with. Still, there was something about the way Madonna responded to being desired, as if she was actively courting it.

I was beginning to see something that I would not understand until years later. Madonna was addicted to attention and enough seemed never to be enough.

From this particular period would come the nudes that later appeared in *Playboy* and *Penthouse* magazines. These shots display someone who already seemed to know that she was an icon. There is one particularly memorable photograph where she is crouching over a small cat, inscrutable as the Sphinx, with her great leonine mane crowning her head. It's strange to imagine for a moment that Madonna had serious concerns that the existence of those photographs would hurt her when they were released after she had made it. None of the photos published was the least bit prurient or suggestive as far as I can see. Initially upset by their appearance, Madonna would quickly realize that in most cases, all publicity was good, particularly for one such as her.

After class, we wandered down West Broadway and stopped in a café for an espresso and a chance for Madonna to indulge her sweet tooth. "So, that guy in the class that you gave your number to, the guy with the camera. Are you going to pose for him?" I asked.

" Maybe. He offered me twenty five dollars an hour."

"Best be careful of who takes your picture. Old photographs can come back to haunt you."

"Should I be worried that someone will blackmail me when I'm rich and famous?" she laughed.

"That woman Eva is from the *Art Student's League*," I said. "Did she ask you to pose privately for her? Everyone says that she's a lesbian."

"Really, Yuck!"

"What's the matter? You have something against gay women?"

"No!" Madonna exclaimed. "As a matter of fact, a girlfriend taught me how to tongue kiss, but Eva is creepy."

Leaving the bistro, we strolled on talking or being silent, in a timeless, dreamlike state, relishing the vibe of artistic ultra hipness that emanated from the streets. Downtown, one could feel the changes in style that would soon impact the rest of the planet. The gaudy colors of the disco seventies were disappearing, replaced by a darker palette dominated by black. Seen just a year before in John Travolta's star vehicle, *Saturday Night Fever*, gaudy platform shoes and polyester bell bottoms were giving way to combat boots, leather jackets and black stovepipe jeans. Hair on men was growing decidedly shorter and moustaches were disappearing as well. To observe the change that would occur over the next ten years one only need look at the top grossing superhero movie that had opened that year of 1978, the brightly garbed *Superman*, and contrast it with one that appeared a decade later, the dark and cynical *Batman.*

Of all the areas of New York, during that period, it felt like Madonna belonged in Soho. Walking down those streets that even at midday always seemed to be wreathed in shadow, people stared at her as if she were a strange exotic creature, although the area was filled with many other quirky and unusual individuals that passed unnoticed. One evening we went to a small hole in the wall Soho club to see a band, *The Lounge Lizards.* Their sound was a mix of tongue-in-cheek jazz styling, combined with new-wave, or as the group described themselves, No Wave rock. Madonna and I both loved *The Lounge Lizards.* The group's sound seemed to perfectly sum up the somewhat detached and ironic "too cool for words" Soho vibe. The room was too small for dancing, but Madonna, practically unable to sit still for music, moved to the quirky jazz beat while still in her seat.

After the show, we headed east and uptown. Madonna turned to me and said, "What I like most about this town is that you can turn a corner and end up in a totally different universe."

We crossed Houston Street and headed up West Broadway, passing chic galleries displaying the latest in modern art. We turned left on 8th Street, which was lined with boutiques and record stores. Madonna looked contemptuously at the clothes in the windows.

"Bridge and Tunnel crap!" she said, referring to the fashion taste of squares from the outer boroughs. I had to laugh, seeing how the recent New York immigrant Madonna was already associating herself with the hippest of the lower Manhattan set.

Crossing East Broadway, 8th Street became St. Marks Place, and the looks displayed in the window were quite different. The stores were already beginning to favor punk rock styles, clothes adorned with skulls, metal studs and spikes with leather bondage decoration. This area was and still is known as the East Village, but it bordered a section then referred to as Alphabet City because the avenues east of 1st were not numbered but given the letters A, B and C as they approached the East River. In 1979, this was still a potentially dangerous neighborhood, inhabited by scores of drug dealers and users, as well as bohemians moving further east in search of affordable housing. It was one of the last sections of Manhattan that would be gentrified. At some point early on in residence in New York, Madonna had lived there, but I was never sure just when this period was, as I could not reconcile it in my own timeline.

Supposedly at this time, Madonna's father Tony had visited her in her East Village apartment and was appalled by the squalor of her dwelling. Horribly, she had also been raped at knifepoint somewhere at some time in that neighborhood, although she had never told that story to me.

She seemed as comfortable and at ease there as any place in New York, a city that fit her like a glove. We stepped inside a boutique called *Trash and Vaudeville*, and Madonna bought a tight spandex zebra-striped tank top. The young salesman eyed her appreciatively in her new skin. As she dressed, I stood next to the large bay window that looked out onto St. Marks Place. I had the sudden strange sensation that I was an actor in a movie, and it was Madonna's movie. It was such a peculiar moment, leaving such a powerful impression that the memory returned to me years later while watching Madonna's calculated documentary, *Truth or Dare*. It was during the sequence when Warren Beatty observed that there would be no point for Madonna to do anything "Off Camera" that it came to me. It was the recollection of that realization that Madonna had practically always behaved as if she was onscreen in her own movie, and that being with her even back then, before her fame, felt as if I was a co-star in that film. The startling fact was that nearly everyone that I had observed around her behaved that way as well.

Seeing how much attention Madonna was receiving, I was fairly certain that I was not the only man in her life. There was nothing that I could specifically put my finger on, except the fact that she was extremely flirtatious. Something about the way she related to men suggested that she enjoyed being the sexual aggressor. She had come on strongly to me, and it had been a turn-on, but in retrospect it had seemed almost macho. In a way, it often felt as if we were similar types, adventurous and constantly trying to push the envelope, but I quickly realized that she was dancing to the beat of a drummer that I could never hope to keep up with.

Still I was sufficiently infatuated with Madonna to imagine that romance with her was possible, and my ego or perhaps something else kept insisting that I was different. "I wasn't just one of a legion of her lovers," I told myself. "We had surely connected on a deeper level that no one else could touch." I would never know if this in fact was true.

One night, I took her to the movies to see a charming film called *A Little Romance*, which was a light comedy, set in Paris with a finale on Venice's Bridge of Sighs. After the movie was over we sat in a café talking about it. Madonna was again wistful.

"I really want to go to Paris. I love Hemmingway's book, *A Moveable Feast*. It's his memoir, set in 1920's Paris. It's all bohemian café society, with Picasso and Gertrude Stein, Ezra Pound and F. Scott Fitzgerald. It's the world that I want to live in."

"I don't think that Paris is like that anymore," I replied. "I think you'll have better luck here in New York."

It was conversations like this that made me realize that I had never known anyone quite like her before. It wasn't that she did or said anything particularly unusual. It was the way in which she seemed to know that what she said would come to pass.

Born in 1958, Madonna was essentially on the outward

cusp of the baby boom. Turning ten in 1968, she certainly would have had an affinity with the 60's Zeitgeist of freedom of expression and artistic exuberance. A part of her was scornful of the hippie movement, because growing up in Bay City Michigan she had seen many of the stoner crowd in her hometown as drug-addled losers with no ambition. Even with that degree of cynicism, Madonna was, like many of those born in the same decade, a romantic. Her association with the world of young Hemmingway's Paris was directly related to the 60s generation's quest for artistic purity. It was the notion that when the artist was hitting the bull's eye, there was basically no separation between that person and their art. Madonna was striving to embody that principle. In that moment, I believed that she would become the next Isadora Duncan, the wild and fiery exhibitionist star of the 1920's who is often cited as the first truly modern dancer. In a sense, that was a notion not too wide off the mark, as Madonna would forge a style of hybrid dance, including ballet, modern, hip-hop and disco moves that would meld with music and revolutionize performance.

I'd known many strange women in my time. Madonna, however, seemed as if she was not quite of this Earth. She was more of a spirit, or what I would come to call an elemental. As a being of pure energy, a force beyond morality and unbound by the laws of nature, her potential seemed unlimited. At other times I scoffed at my silly notions. She was merely a girl, bluffing her way along, scared and far from home. What did I know, anyway? As time passed I would come to know just how accurate my perceptions were.

CHAPTER SIX
"MARLON BRANDO, JIMMIE DEAN, ON THE COVER OF A MAGAZINE. VOGUE."
–MADONNA, 1990

Madonna has oft invited comparison to Marilyn Monroe, but the person that she most identified with at that time was James Dean, the ultimate fast fuse rebel. One night, we went to the movies to see *Midnight Express*, starring Brad Davis.

"He looks so much like James Dean!" she said. "I'm obsessed with James Dean. He's so tender and tough at the same time. Did you know that he lost his mother as a kid? Just like me. When that happens, you realize that if you can stand to lose the thing that you love the most and survive, you can handle anything. Dean died when he was twenty-four. I think that I'll be dead before I'm thirty, like my mother."

I was stunned. This was the first she had told me of this. In that moment my heart went out to her. Her mother died when she was just five years old. That explained the sense of yearning that enveloped her. It also explained the tough exterior and the tenderness inside. I asked her to tell me a bit more about her mother. She stared down at her hands for what seemed to be a long time and then suddenly looked up at me.

"My mother was beautiful, like an angel. She was named Madonna too. She died of breast cancer. I was too young to really understand. When I look at Dean, I recognize the look in his eyes. Like you've lost something that you can't bear to lose... but you know that you can never get it back."

As she was speaking, it occurred to me that there was the

romantic attachment to death there somewhere. Would James Dean be as popular if he had lived to be 80, rather than wiping out at 90 mph in his Porsche on a lonely stretch of highway? Was Madonna afraid of dying young, or did part of her secretly want to?

The next day, I bought her a large coffee table book of Dennis Stock's fabulous photographs of Dean. The actor had taken Stock to his family's Indiana farm and to his favorite New York stomping grounds. Madonna zeroed in on one particular shot. Dean was shuffling down the middle of Broadway near Times Square in the rain. No one else appeared to be on the street. He was the solitary star, surrounded by the oppressive vastness of the Great White Way. He was isolated, accompanied only by his reflection in the rain soaked streets.

"That's exactly how if felt when I got to New York," she said. "The cabdriver took me to Times Square, and I walked around with my bags for hours."

There it was again. It was the romantic association of alienation and pain with the life of a true artist. Of course Madonna had felt lost and lonely on her own in New York, but she also seemed to be enjoying her ennobling isolation.

The next day, Madonna had a present for me. It was her battered copy of Hemmingway's *A Moveable Feast*.

A few days later I went to the movies alone to watch James Dean in *East of Eden*, based on John Steinbeck's novel set in the Salinas Valley of California. Dean's character, Cal Trask seemed to mirror the tragedy of the actor's youth. Abandoned by his wicked and venal mother at his birth, Cal Trask was an open wound of seething resentment and bitterness. Dean's stunningly physical and verbally inarticulate portrayal of the character was almost too painful to watch. It was no wonder that Madonna had been drawn to his somewhat androgynous appeal. Like Pearl Lang's tortured style of dancing, Dean's acting was angst-ridden.

Dean's Method acting style was an integral part of a movement led by the Russian teacher Stanislavski and his disciples, Stella Adler and Lee Strasberg. Dean's second film, *Rebel Without a Cause* had a strong appeal for alienated teenagers, particularly after the actor died before the movie was released. By doing so, he seemed to perfectly embody the ideal of beat poet Jack Kerouac as he expressed it so clearly in his novel, *On the Road*.

"The only people for me are the mad ones, the ones who are mad to live, mad to talk, mad to be saved, desirous of everything at the same time, the ones who never yawn or say a commonplace thing, but burn, burn, burn, like fabulous yellow roman candles exploding like spiders across the stars and in the middle you see the blue centerlight pop and everybody goes "Awww!"

This could easily be seen as Madonna's philosophy as well.

Dean was also considered an Icon among the gay and bi-sexual population, particularly in New York and Hollywood. Warhol drag queen actor and former *Max's Kansas City* habitué Jackie Curtis was also obsessed with the actor. Curtis has since been immortalized in the Lou Reed song, *Take a Walk on the Wild Side*, with the lyric, *"She thought she was James Dean for a day."*

Although hailing from the Midwest, both of the quintessential film method actors, James Dean and Marlon Brando, epitomize the gritty reality, raw physicality and intellectual curiosity of New York. Scores of actors and musicians in the metropolis owe a debt to the legacies of the twin titans of the Method. As someone strongly affected by the Brando magnetism, I was no exception. I was enormously flattered that Madonna thought that I resembled Brando. He and Dean were the ultimate rebels, and there seemed to be so much to rebel against.

CHAPTER SEVEN
IRVING PLAZA

Christmas came and I did not see Madonna for about ten days. She called me on a Thursday, asking if I wanted to take her to a dance club called *Irving Plaza*. She had moved house again, this time to the West Village, with a roommate named Susan. They lived in a high-rise apartment complex, whose courtyard featured a huge concrete Picasso sculpture. When Madonna opened the front door, without warning she leaped forward, trusting that I would catch her. She proceeded to climb up me as if I were a tree, covering me with hot wet kisses. Without undressing, we coupled on the living room floor in a wild heat of passion.

In this case, sex was merely a prelude to the main event.

Madonna was bursting with energy and very anxious to hit the dance floor. She was a woman of many moods and I was learning to be prepared for whichever one might manifest. That evening she was the girl that Warren Beatty would someday nickname "Buzz bomb."

We got on the building's elevator, singing together the Donna Summer hit song, "*How's about some Hot Stuff, baby this evening. I want some Hot Stuff, baby tonight!*" at the top of our lungs. The couple already on board stared at us in disbelief. They were decked out like a couple of middle-aged Las Vegas rubes. The man had a greasy black pompadour and a pencil thin moustache. He wore a bright blue sharkskin jacket with a string bolo tie, fastened with a silver steer skull. The woman wore a red crinoline mini dress under a silver fox fur coat. She had peroxide blonde hair and eyelashes like Tammy Faye Baker. Madonna was wearing her leopard tights and a black leather motorcycle jacket. She had trimmed her bushy hair and swept it back. She looked very new wave.

"Hey, you two sound good together!" the man said to me as he leaned casually against the elevator door.

"I'm Larry. This is my wife, Roz. Where are you and your punk girlfriend off to?"

"Uh, we're going dancing at *Irving Plaza*," I replied.

We exited the building, heading towards Bleecker Street. Larry gestured towards the curb. "Hop in our limo. We'll give you a lift over."

The limo was furnished as tackily as its owners, and of course featured a full bar. Larry poured each of us a flute of champagne. "So...we're going to Atlantic City, to a few casinos. How'd ya like to party with us?"

"I don't know. Maybe," I replied. "Madonna, what do you think?"

She looked at me, dubiously. Then leaned over and hissed in my ear.

"No fucking way, man. These guys are lame. We're not going anywhere with them. We are going dancing."

"No thanks," I said to Larry. "We'll get out at *Irving Plaza*."

Inside the club, the dance floor was spacious. *Irving Plaza* had only re-opened a year earlier and already had a reputation as one of the hippest New-Wave dance clubs in town. The DJ was spinning cutting edge music: *The Clash, Talking Heads, The Specials* and *The B52's*. Occasionally, he mixed in something stranger. Suddenly, the DJ was playing Nancy Sinatra's "These Boots Are Made For Walkin.'"

"Oh, My God!" Madonna screamed. "This is my absolute favorite song!"

She began singing along enthusiastically and several people on the floor turned to listen to her appreciatively and watch her wild jungle cat moves. Madonna was cutting loose totally, fully utilizing the space. She was doing her spin-into Grand jeté move that was so astounding. She then proceeded to perform a series of leaps from one end of the floor to the other. When the music slowed down, I found myself doing a slow mambo grind with her. As I held her around her waist, she arched back, bringing her head to the floor, whereupon I swept her around and around dizzily. The lighting engineer turned a blue spot on us, and suddenly we had become the show. Madonna lifted her legs, hooking her feet around my neck while I kept a hold on her hips, continuing to sweep her in a slow circle as her long dark hair brushed the dance floor. I was discovering that I was capable of remarkable dexterity and was learning a good many improvisational moves in an effort to keep up with Madonna's need to show off her extroverted creativity.

On this night, as always, I was aware of other people's responses to her. Several times, when I'd left her alone for a moment, I would return to find her in conversation with another man. Once I had seen her passing a man a slip of paper, possibly with her phone number on it. Had I been the least bit possessive, I could have easily been driven out of my mind with jealousy by the barrage of advances towards her. At this point I had decided that since our days together were probably numbered, it would be best not to do anything to cramp her style. Down the rabbit hole and through the looking glass the rules are different. I would hang on and enjoy the ride, and not attempt to coerce the wild child that I had momentarily tethered.

CHAPTER EIGHT
HELL'S KITCHEN AND THE
VENETIAN DREAM

Madonna moved yet again. She was now in a tenement walk up apartment on 9th Avenue in the west forties, an area known as Hell's Kitchen. Just a few blocks across town from Times Square, it had none of the pizzazz of the entertainment hub. It was an area with little charm, lacking even the neighborhood flavor of the lower East side or Harlem. The buildings were old and not well kept. Someone had painted a menagerie of jungle animals on the building's façade. It was appropriate for several reasons. The neighborhood had the feel of an asphalt jungle, wild and untamed, and the leopard girl lived upstairs.

That afternoon, she was sullen and unresponsive. She was listening to David Bowie's *The Rise and Fall of Ziggy Stardust and the Spiders From Mars*. She adored Bowie, but this was not exactly romantic music and I was in an amorous mood.

When I moved close to her, she shunned my caresses. Then, somewhat listlessly, she responded. It felt as if she was going through the motions, either out of habit or just to please me, but she did not seem emotionally engaged. When we had finished with our uninspired lovemaking, I felt none of the blissful afterglow that I'd experienced on other occasions with her. I simply felt the emptiness of a futile act of lust. I stared out of the window at the starkness of 9th Avenue, depressed and unable to communicate why it was so.

My negative feelings for the neighborhood seemed reflected in Madonna's coldness toward me. She felt like an alien. I asked her if she was seeing anyone else.

"I don't want to talk about it. It's none of your business."

"Well, you didn't really feel very warm to me. Are you tired of me?"

"No, I just not always in the mood. It's not you."

I didn't believe her. Something had changed inside of her and inside of me as well.

I thought about my feelings on my walk uptown. During the last several times that we had been together I was beginning to feel increasingly annoyed by her propensity to test the people around her. She seemed to enjoy pushing buttons, saying or doing something just to elicit a response. Although she was erudite, with an extensive vocabulary, Madonna enjoyed being vulgar and would use profanity in inappropriate situations. It was clearly for shock value, as she done years later during her appearance on *David Letterman's Late Show*, when she had repeatedly used the word "fuck." Such behavior was beginning to make me feel uncomfortable rather than amusing me as it did previously.

But it was something else that was disturbing me. On the first night we made love, I was struck by the depth of her passion and the completeness of her surrender. From that point on I noticed that she was gradually withdrawing from me. Was she afraid that she had been touched too deeply? Was she now putting up a wall to distance herself from the force of that emotion?

A few nights later, I had a strange and prophetic dream. Madonna and I were walking along a river embankment. Around us there was an exquisite Venetian dreamscape of villas and footbridges, enveloped in fog. Gradually, I became aware that it was no longer Madonna at my side, but an enormous lion. As I sat upon the ground, the cat rested its head in my lap, nuzzling my groin. Then suddenly, the cat sprang up and gazed searchingly into my eyes. After what felt like an eternity, the lion turned and padded silently off into the mists.

Years later when I first saw Madonna's "Like a Virgin" video, I was stunned. The film had practically recreated my leonine Venetian dream.

The dream sent a clear message to my subconscious mind. Madonna was too wild and independent for me to hold onto. Sooner or later, like the lion in the dream she would leave me. The time to chase after elusive elementals was over. I decided not to call Madonna for a while. Her coolness towards me was a clear indication of her disinterest. If I was wrong about that, then I would hear from her, but I did not.

My dancer friend Michael had just introduced me to a woman named Marge, and she and I had started dating. She was sweet and uncomplicated compared to Madonna, and it felt like a relief not to have to second-guess her. A few weeks later, I had almost forgotten Madonna.

CHAPTER NINE
TRIBECA AND CORONA

For several years since I'd had my own apartment, I had enjoyed the tradition of throwing a party on the first of May. This had nothing to do with the Communist labor holiday, but everything to do with the ancient pagan rite of spring tradition to observe the renewal of life. Pagans celebrated wanton sexuality, and children born from the revelries were considered children of May because they were often ignorant of their patrimony. My celebration was considerably more chaste, but fun and festive, particularly in the spring of 1979, with the cooperation of Dan Gilroy and Bernard Roth's theatrical crowd. The party was to be held in a large Tribeca loft that was the workplace of my current girlfriend, Marge. Tribeca is another compound word to describe a neighborhood, this time signifying the triangle below Canal Street. It was another formerly industrial neighborhood that had been occupied by artists after Soho had grown too pricy.

I had not seen Madonna for several months. It was the fickle finger of fate that put me in her path while walking on West 34th street. I felt the rush of memories of her hit me as I stood on the crowded sidewalk trying to collect my thoughts. It felt great to see her again. She looked fantastic. She had cut her hair in a sort of pageboy and she was wearing a white denim jacket and tight black jeans.

"Hey N.B., how've you been?" she said. She gestured at my tight t-shirt "You've lost some weight. Your body has more definition. Looks nice."

I moved in and kissed her lightly on the cheek. I wanted to hold her, but I was playing it cool. I thought of Marge, my girlfriend, and held myself away from Madonna's magnetism.

"I'm good, Madonna. You know, I was just thinking about you. How are you? How's the dance world?"

"I quit!"

I was momentarily at a loss for words, stammering.

"What do you mean, you quit?"

"I quit studying with Pearl. I went to class one day and we were working on a performance piece that I was supposed to have a part in. I felt like I was in a museum of antiquities. It just didn't feel relevant any more."

I didn't know what to say. As far as I was concerned, Madonna's life was dance. How could she have simply quit?

"So what are you going to do now?"

"I dunno. Maybe music."

" OK, well listen, I'm throwing a party next week and you are someone I'd love to see there. A lot of artists, musicians, your kind of people."

"Sounds groovy!" she said enthusiastically. "Give me the address. I'll be sure to come."

Somehow, the word got out that our party was the place to be that night. The loft was full of colorful and enthusiastic people and the music was pumping. The crowd was mixed and eclectic: A very gay element mixed with rock n' rollers and Bohemian artists. One of the guests had taken the spring theme seriously and was decked out in a leaf ensemble, covering his head and loins with shrubbery.

Madonna arrived. I realized that I had been anticipating possibly seeing her again all day. I hadn't been sure she that she would come. She was dressed in two T-shirts and black *Danskin* tights. She gave me the warm hug of a long lost friend, and feeling at home, she immediately began to mingle. As host, I felt obliged to attend to our guests, so after introducing her to my co-host Dan, I moved off into the crowd. Later on I noticed them together. I sauntered over to eavesdrop on their conversation. They were talking about music and how there were a lot of exciting new bands around. Madonna joked that she wanted to start a band and call it The 80s. She and Dan walked over to the sound system, and Madonna told the guy pretending to be the DJ to play more New Wave music. The DJ put on "Rock Lobster" by *The B52's* and Madonna was temporarily mollified. When Gloria Gaynor's disco anthem, "I Will Survive" came on, Madonna was right in the groove. She screamed out the words with a defiance that suggested that this was more than just a song to her.

I could see that the attraction between Dan and Madonna was instantaneous. Dan's laid -back sense of humor was an immediate turn on for Madonna. Later, she would say that what immediately impressed her about him was his naturalness. In a world of men that Madonna had known, so many of them tried to come off as drop-dead cool. Dan was just Dan. What you saw was what you got. This wasn't completely accurate however. Dan was one of the smartest people I've known and there were many layers to the man.

Later in the evening, as I was dancing with Marge, I saw Dan and Madonna in the corner, kissing. I was instantly seized by powerful pangs of jealousy. I tried vainly to push them aside, but it was to no avail. "What was the matter with me?" I thought. I was going steady with a nice sensible girl. Danny was one of my favorite people; he and Madonna seemed nearly perfect for each other at that moment. But I couldn't help but realize that Dan and I were back to our old pattern. Here he was getting interested in a woman I'd recently broken up with.

Little did I realize that this was a pivotal period in Madonna's life. At the precise moment that Madonna was preparing to abandon the rigors of a professional dance career, fate had delivered to her the man that would give her the confidence to leap into the unknown world of musical performance. When Madonna first visited Danny at the "Gog" in Corona, Queens, she stepped into the realm of the band rehearsal space, where she would soon be completely at home. Madonna was introduced to a world where musicians honed their instrumental talents and their compositions as she had previously honed her body with the rigors of dance.

From that point onward, events moved quickly, as if planned. Through Bernard Roth's theatrical connections, Dan and Ed were featured in a satirical musical review of their creation, called *Voidville*. The brothers were hard at work rehearsing as *The Bill and Gil Show* with Madonna as an appreciative audience. As Bill and Gil, Dan and Ed combined rock n' roll with their own distinctive brand of comedy, using routines that they had played since childhood. The two brothers had always been close and had the chemistry of old best friends.

When *Voidville* opened, early performances were seen by a pair of European producers looking for back up performers for their star, disco singer Patrick Hernandez, who had just had a hit with, "Born to Be Alive." Dan informed Madonna that the producers, Jan Van Lieu and Claude Pellerin were holding open auditions for the Hernandez review.

Madonna made a strong impression on the producers. Rather than using her as simply another body in the Hernandez review, they offered to set her up in Paris, grooming her to be the next Edith Piaf. Early that summer, Madonna flew to Paris, land of her Hemmingway artistic fantasy.

I was excited for Madonna. It seemed that her dreams of stardom were about to come true in a place that she had always longed to go to. I was also sad to see her go, not knowing if I would ever see her again. I had broken up with Marge over the summer and was romantically adrift. I was beginning to wonder if I was as restless as Madonna. I did not seem to know what I wanted out of a relationship, and I was missing the excitement of being with the exquisite elemental again.

News came to me of Madonna in Paris via Danny. After a few months of grooming and pampering in Van Lieu and

Pellerin's stable, Madonna had had enough. She felt as if she were a robot, working out the mechanical routines that the producers were putting her through. Dan was also busy doing his part to woo her back, sending Madonna droll postcards telling her how much she was missed. In late July, Madonna told her Belgian bosses that she needed a few weeks to visit her family. She got a round trip ticket to the States and split the Parisian scene, returning to New York to resume her musical odyssey with the Gilroy brothers.

CHAPTER TEN
WEST 69TH STREET

During this period, I was drawn back into the *CBGB* music scene when I got a phone call from my old guitarist friend Ritchie Fleigler, who had spent the last year touring with Lou Reed, a singer from the musically influential Warhol sponsored group *Velvet Underground*. Ritchie had played with Ed Gilroy and me several years ago. He was bristling with newfound confidence due to his time spent on the road.

"Terry Ork wants to record some new acts for his Indie label. I suggested he record you," Ritchie said.

"Yeah," I replied. "I know Ork from Max's. He's *Television's* manager. Who's going to be in the studio?"

"Well, I'll be on guitar, Bruce Brody from Patty Smith's band will be on keyboards and I think Fred Smith and Jesse Chamberlain."

"Sounds good!" I said. "Count me in!"

Several days later, I showed up for the session. We were recording a cover version of an old R&B tune called, "I Feel Like Rockin' All the Time" for the A side, and the old Junior Welles/Buddy Guy cut, "Messin' With The Kid" as the B- side. The session went well. Terry Ork was enthusiastic.

"We all know about New Wave. Well this here is the Blue Wave! We'll call you *Blue Norris.*"

The appropriate documents were produced and signed. A month later, a press release appeared in a music paper called *The New York Rocker*, announcing the impending release of the record by the fabulous Norris Burroughs.

That record was never released. Ork was overextended financially and didn't have the resources to follow through on his promises. I was crushed. It felt like the rug had been yanked out from under me. I was beginning to see how hard it was to make something happen in the real world. I did a few gigs with Fliegler's All Star band, and that was the end of that. We even played *CBGB* along with *Television's* guitarist Richard Lloyd to an enthusiastic crowd. However, I got the strong impression that blues inflected rock music was again simply not punk enough for the scene.

I moved house as well, leaving the sterility and plasticity of the Upper East Side for the warmer neighborhood of west 69th near Central Park West. I began going to a local restaurant called *The Saloon*, which became a killer pick-up joint for me. I was spending my weekends at the Ocean Bay Park community on Fire Island, where the singles scene was rocking and the drug of choice was Quaalude, which often had the happy side effect of erasing the memory of the previous night's debauch. 1979, in my mind, was the high water mark for the swinging singles era; happening at the height of disco, just before the twin curses of herpes and AIDS reared their ugly heads. Never before and never again would I witness the plethora of sexually predatory women that arose during that period, as I was repeatedly treated as a disposable sex toy. One Sunday, under the blistering Fire Island sun, I met a young woman with a striking resemblance to Madonna and attached myself to her. After some time drinking and kissing, I became wistful. I realized that the memory of the Elemental was still with me.

CHAPTER ELEVEN
LIFE IN THE GOG

Madonna phoned me shortly after returning from France. She had gotten my new phone number from Dan. Needless to say, I was happy to hear from her and more than pleasantly surprised that she had tracked me down. I could hear the warmth in her voice.

"Hey there N.B. I'm starring in a film. We're shooting a scene in a limo in your neighborhood today. Why don't you come by and give me a neck massage?"

The film was being shot a few blocks north, on Broadway. It would eventually become the notoriously cheesy movie, *A Certain Sacrifice*, which would return to haunt Madonna years later when it was released just as she was becoming a superstar.

I bought Madonna a cappuccino and tapped on the window of the stretch limo parked in front of *the Beacon Theater* on 74th and Broadway. She opened the door and pulled me inside the spacious back seat, giving me a warm, passionate kiss. She was wearing full makeup and a black tuxedo jacket with something very sheer underneath. She looked stunning.

"I have a present for you," she said.

"Really, what is it?"

"Here, it's a leotard that used to belong to my brother Chris. You love dancers so much. I think that you should study."

I accepted the black danskin top dubiously. It looked a bit small, but I could probably use it on stage for something.

"Madonna, I'm twenty-seven years old. How am I going to become a dancer now?"

"Hey, once a dancer, always a dancer."

There was no one else in the car but the driver up front. I

massaged the tension from her shoulders as she updated me on her life.

"I've moved in with Dan Gilroy. I'm playing music with *The Breakfast Club* now. Mostly drums. I'm singing two numbers in the set. Not mine, although I am writing some songs."

"Let's hear a song," I challenged.

She proceeded to sing a portion of a tune called "Hothouse Flower."

"*Don't come around and try to break my bubble. I'm a Hothouse Flower, yeah I stay by myself everyday.*"

"It sounds sad, like you're a little bit lonely," I replied.

"No way, man. I'm really happy. I really like living in Corona. It's like a real neighborhood. It reminds me a little of back home in Michigan."

Madonna pointed out the window to the nearby theater marquee.

"Joe Jackson is playing tonight. Wanna go?"

"Sorry, I already have plans. How did you like Paris?"

"It was OK. They took me to Tunisia, Belgium... I felt like a bird in a gilded cage. I took off. I just had to get away. I don't want someone to make me into their idea of what they think is hot. You know, I think that you were right. I think that what I was looking for is happening right here. Paris is too old, too decadent. New York is the happening place right now."

Madonna was right. New York was exploding, blossoming with hot new clubs. Joining *CBGB* as a premier punk venue was the notorious *Mudd Club*, which catered to punk as well as early hip-hop, reggae music and ska. *The Mudd Club* was a study in grunge, with an iron pipe running along the wall.

By 1980, *Danceteria* and *the Ritz* would open in lower Manhattan. There were dozens of venues where Madonna would play, once she had started performing, including a sanitized version of Max's that had reopened in the old location. When I visited the club and walked to the back room, I got none of the sense of exclusivity that one felt from the space five years ago. No one was holding court and no one there seemed to be invested with an aura of "Cool." The back room just felt like an ordinary dining area, no different from the front. Nor did there appear to be any style evident there. That was not necessarily a bad thing however. There was an eclectic mix of styles, with no one predominant.

That seemed to also be the case in the music scene in general, where experimentation was the operating word. Although on the surface there seemed to be a conflict between styles of music, say punk and disco, new hybrid forms of music were evolving directly from the streets. Rap, or hip-hop, was making headway, and that wild girl, Deborah Harry, had again been audacious enough to include a nonsensical take off on the new music, which she called "Rapture." Harry and her street-smart musical partner Chris Stein were always on the lookout for new styles and ideas to take the group in new directions, and this gamble paid off. In the song's video, graffiti artist *Fab Five Freddy* was featured and the song's lyric referenced up-and-coming rapper *Grandmaster Flash.*

Madonna was definitely paying attention. Although she appeared to resent *Blondie*, it was simply jealousy. She actually admired Deborah Harry. It was just that Madonna wanted to be the cutting edge Queen of Punk, and if she had her way, it wouldn't be long before she was.

I took the 7 Train to Corona early one Saturday morning in the late summer of 1979, to see what *The Breakfast Club* was up to. It was literally breakfast, at the International House of Pancakes, where the gang went to carb and coffee up for their afternoon rehearsal. Madonna and Dan were both vegetarians, but enjoyed their eggs. Pancakes with plenty of maple syrup were something that we all could agree on.

Returning to the Synagogue, which the inhabitants referred to as the "*Gog*" the band settled into rehearsing one of Eddie's tunes. Madonna's beautiful dancer friend Angie

Smit was playing bass and none too well, while Madonna hammered out a rudimentary drumbeat. She played drums enthusiastically, with a natural sense of syncopation honed by years of using her body as an instrument. She seemed to focus on the snare drum and Tom-Tom, using the cymbals sparingly. Then, she practiced using the bass drum pedal to keep a steady beat.

After several takes of the song, Dan sat with Madonna to teach her to play the guitar chords for the next song, something that Dan had written called "Moving Along." She had pretty much mastered the song already, and she then stood up to perform it, with Dan backing her on drums and Ed playing a few lead guitar accent licks. As she did with the drums, Madonna played guitar with her whole body, like the dancer that she was. She bounced on the balls of her feet, moving up, down and sideways to the beat. What she lacked in technique, she made up for with enthusiastic body language.

Dan and Ed, as rock n' rollers, tended to play a lot of bar chords, using the forefinger as a capo while keeping the other fingers in the E chord position and then moving up and down the guitar neck. This is an easy way to play rudimentary guitar, and along with the drums it was the foundation of Madonna's musical education. Prior to the day that Danny taught her to play bar chords, she had never realized that she herself could also write music. That moment was a turning point in her life. She began to write a song each day. She also started to play the keyboard again, using Dan's old electric Farfisa organ. In rehearsal, Madonna seemed comfortable although she was not particularly assertive. She seemed be aware that she was in a sort of apprenticeship, and she was respectful and attentive to Dan and Eddie's musical leadership. Her relationship with Dan seemed to be affectionate but as a couple they were not overly demonstrative around others. Seeing their coolness, it gave me the unrealistic sense that perhaps they were not that committed to a romantic relationship. As a result of this observation, I had it in my mind that perhaps I could gradually win my way back to her heart.

Over that fall and winter leading into 1980, I was often at Breakfast Club rehearsals, sometimes joining them for four mile runs around Flushing Meadow Park. The park is spacious, having been the location for the 1964 Worlds Fair. Still standing from the exposition were the Unisphere, which is a huge steel globe, and the towering New York State Pavilion, which is still a performance venue.

The neighborhood was pleasant, with a profusion of trees as well as its proximity to the park. It also was well integrated: a lower middle class mix of Italians, Irish, African Americans, Afro-Caribbeans, Hispanics and Asians. It felt wholesome and comfortable in Corona.

As mentioned, the rehearsal space was the main body of the Synagogue, with its altar or bimah still standing. The room was spacious with good acoustics for performance. Because of the prominence of the bimah, the space exuded an aura of majesty, as if something of importance was occurring there. The sun flooded into the large room and highlighted the beauty of the carved wood and gold structure.

Madonna flirted with me openly during the rehearsal, but I kept my distance except for an occasional caress. I didn't want to create any unnecessary tension and I figured that my time might come around again if I played my cards right. It was certain that I hadn't gotten over her completely, and the fact that she was with Dan was not a sufficient deterrent to me. After all, he and I had been down that route before. What I didn't know but should have realized was how completely he'd fallen for her as well.

One afternoon during a break, Madonna and I walked down the block and around the corner to a local bakery that served coffee and Italian pastries. I bought her a cannoli and an espresso and we walked outside, eating our delicacies. Noticing that she had powdered sugar on her chin, I leaned forward and gently brushed the sugar from her mouth.

"You're covered with sugar, as usual," I said.

I moved closer and kissed her behind her ear.

"I love you. I always will."

"Ditto," she replied.

CHAPTER TWELVE
GOSSAMER WING

One morning, Dan brought Madonna to *Gossamer Wing*, the textile design company where he and I worked. As one of the principals in the company, he had agreed to give her some part time work painting the runs of fabric. The Wing was a large loft space on West 39thStreet with ample room for several ten-foot tables. Dan led her over to the long wooden structures, stretched with ten yards of China silk.

"We draw the resist outline in hot wax, tracing the shape from the light box underneath," he explained as he demonstrated. Fellow designers Bernard, Maureen, Jan and I stood watching, as Madonna picked up the tjanting tool and dipped it into the pot of bubbling liquid wax. She withdrew it, and attempted to trace a line onto the taut silk surface. Her first attempt failed, spilling blobs of wax across the silk. After several tries, she gave up, flustered.

"Come back in an hour," Danny said, sympathetically. "We'll wax the run and you can try painting it."

Madonna was more successful at painting, filling in the shapes enclosed by the now solid wax lines with silk dye. Later that day, during my lunch break, I was sitting alone in a small storage room, practicing on my acoustic guitar when Madonna walked in. "What are you practicing?" she asked.

'Oh, it's a series of scales I learned from my guitar teacher. When I didn't have them down at my lesson the other day, I made excuses and my teacher said that I was being petulant."

"I love that word. People have called me that, but I didn't take it as an insult. I felt like they were saying that I was a brat, but totally charming."

"That about sums you up," I said.

From that day forth, I noticed that Madonna also practiced the guitar in the back room during her lunch break. One day I wandered in, to find her singing and playing a song that sounded vaguely familiar.

"Where have I heard that before?" I pondered.

" Nowhere. I just wrote it today."

"That sounds like that Joni Mitchell song, "Marcy," I said.

"Oh Shit, you're right. God damn it." She was crestfallen and momentarily discouraged.

"That's OK. It happens to me all the time. I write something new and then I realize that it's a song already."

Madonna worked at the Wing for several weeks during the autumn of 1979. There was always an up tempo energy while she was there. A crew of about a half a dozen artists worked on the runs, and as we did, we listened to the radio and sang along or made fun of the songs. The *Sugarhill Gang's* "Rapper's Delight" was often played, and we made fools of ourselves trying to imitate the hip-hop tempo. We talked about music constantly.

"Have you heard *The Police*? That guy Sting is cool."

"Check out *Squeeze's* new album, *Argybargy*. They have this great way of doing octave harmonies."

"I love Joe Jackson. He sounds a bit like Elvis Costello."

In late 1979, most of the hip crowd agreed that disco was dead, although it was very much alive. There was still good new dance music being made. Not only that, Europeans like Giorgio Moroder were producing synthesizer based tracks like "Call Me" by *Blondie* that mixed New Wave and disco styles to scintillating effect.

Madonna mentioned that she really liked Prince. No on else at the Wing did at the time. It would take several years for his strange ways to come into favor, but Madonna, with her penchant for the hyper erotic could instantly spot a kindred spirit. Another female singer that appeared to make a strong impression on Madonna was *Fleetwood Mac's* Stevie Nicks, a standout personality in a group full of outstanding talents. Nicks would develop into a formidable solo artist, and her raw but passionate voice and ethereal beauty would be compelling to the impressionable Madonna.

Curtis Zale, one of the artists at *Gossamer Wing*, was particularly fond of all-girl music groups like the *Shangri-Las* and *the Ronettes*. Zale loved *Blondie* and played the group's tape on the loft's cassette player. He immediately began to champion Madonna as a front woman for *The Breakfast Club*. Having a good fashion sense, he also gave Madonna some clothes, which she was able to cleverly combine to create ensemble fashion statements.

One evening, he invited us to a performance of a group that he was enthusiastic about. *Get Wet*, fronted by a diminutive female singer named Sheri Beachfront, had a catchy song called "Which Window" that was getting a bit of airplay on New York radio.

Realizing that her own singing and dancing talents far outweighed Beachfront's, Madonna instantly resented the fact that the *Get Wet* star seemed already on her way to fame and fortune. In the same way that she had been somewhat dismissive of Deborah Harry, Madonna was fiercely competitive with anyone who was already doing what she herself craved intensely. After the show, I asked her what she thought of *Get Wet*.

"Not so hot, They're all wet!" she replied.

One Saturday evening, I held a small party at my West 69th Street digs, inviting Madonna, the Gilroys and various other friends and neighbors. An hour or so into the party, I noticed that Dan and Madonna were in the corner of the room having some sort of disagreement. While they were keeping their voices low, they still seemed to be arguing. Then Dan stood up, agitated and said, "Alright, have it your way. You usually do."

He turned and walked out the door. Madonna didn't seem particularly upset by the altercation. Rickie Lee Jones' debut album was on the turntable and she stood up and began moving slowly to the languid beat of a song called "Coolsville." I left my chair and moved up behind her, maneuvering her into the hallway where I could have her to myself. As the song played, I pressed my hips against her behind, grinding rhythmically. "Mmmmm," she said. "That's my favorite position."

I wanted her badly. I whispered in her ear, "Do you want to stay after everyone else has left?'
"Maybe," she replied.

Danny returned shortly thereafter, shattering my hopes for a romantic interlude. The couple left the party having worked out their differences.

At that moment, I knew that I was doing myself a disservice by behaving this way with Madonna. Whether or not she was capable of remaining faithful to Danny, I realized that as much as I wanted her, I didn't want to be the one to sully their relationship.

CHAPTER THIRTEEN
THE MOTHER LAND

One Saturday at the T-Shirt Gallery, *Finn told me that he wanted me to do a pres*entation of airbrushed Graffiti shirts. I decided to take a field trip up to the Bronx to see what I could find in the way of artistic inspiration. I asked Madonna if she was interested in coming along. She was enthusiastic about the trip, because she was curious about the new hip-hop sounds and styles, but when the day arrived, I could not reach her by phone. I took the number 6 train to Elder Avenue and headed for the Bronx River projects, home of the Godfather of Bronx hip-hop, Afrika Bambaattaa. I didn't expect to see him there, and he was not. What I did see was my first experience of break dancing, as kids in the project were squaring off in a rockin' contest, moving to the beat from a bass heavy boom box. Their agility was astounding as they executed gravity defying somersaults and spins. They eyed me, wondering what the white guy with the camera was doing there. The media hadn't gotten hip to the new grooves yet.

I took a few photos and headed west across Freeman Street under the elevated train that I had traveled in so many times to my parents' home further north. It was the number 2 train, commonly referred to as the "Beast" because of its prominence there, and because of the neighborhoods that it traversed. As a train passed overhead, I took some quick reference shots of the artwork that was spray painted on its sides, and continued north to the 180th Street Yards, where the trains were stored and were sitting targets for graffiti artists. There were scores of cars that had been decorated in "wild style" tag names that were lettered in bizarrely creative angular typefaces. I took a bunch of pictures and headed into Bronx Park. I was now in my old territory, close to where I grew up. Thinking about the gangs of the South Bronx had me thinking about my own youthful gang experience. At age fourteen in 1966, I ran with a gang of boys my age that called themselves *The Young Assassins*. We hung out in the playground across from my home and roamed the sprawling rambles of Bronx Park, emulating the older gangs that terrorized the neighborhood.

What was ironic was that at this very moment of 1979–80 there were two movies playing simultaneously that were bookends to the youth gang life of the city over a twenty-year span. Both these films went on to achieve cult status as movies that seriously evoked a period and a slice of life.

The first was *The Wanderers*, which was a more or less true account of an early sixties Bronx gang. At some point in the film, which was based on the novel by Bronx native Richard Price, *The Wanderers* encountered the more fearsome Bronx gangs that even *the Assassins* were familiar with, *The Fordham Baldies* and the legendary *Ducky Boys*, who were nearly as deadly with their marble loaded slingshots as a modern gang packing heat is.

The second movie is *The Warriors*, which was the tale of a more modern, late 70s Brooklyn gang that must make their way home from the wilds of the Bronx by subway train. The train of course represented the rite of passage, the journey through the underworld. To the gang members, the train was the most powerful aspect of their lives - both their major means of transportation and a powerful symbol of life force. *The Warriors* knew, as did the real South Bronx gangs, that to mark the train with graffiti was the ultimate statement of power.

Having passed through the South Bronx neighborhood on foot, I felt as though I had a greater understanding of the soul of graffiti as an art form, as well as having a better sense of the human nature of an area I had usually regarded with fear and loathing.

On the other hand, like most people at the time, I did not believe for an instant that hip-hop or rap music would be anything but a fly by night fad. To an elitist musician such as I imagined myself to be, rap music seemed simplistic, almost moronic in its insistent repetition and lack of vocal melody.

Over the next decade, as the music and lifestyle gained greater and greater popularity, I was astounded and baffled by its resilience and longevity. The South Bronx, generally perceived as a symbol of urban decay, is seldom celebrated as the fertile ground for the birth of a worldwide phenomenon, but it was so. Hip-hop culture would come to influence Madonna and her musical peers at least as much as the New Wave music that she was focusing on in 1980.

When I returned to the *T-Shirt Gallery* the following week, my head was full of wild ideas and I produced a wall full of colorful urban designs.

The Breakfast Club finally scored a gig at *CBGB*, and I made sure that I was present. The Bowery neighborhood surrounding the club was seriously run down, with winos and lost souls merging with the punk and new wave kids surrounding the place. This section of the Bowery was actually just a few blocks south of St. Marks Place, the heart of the East Village, but the further south you traveled from that point, the more the neighborhood deteriorated. This was the peculiar thing about New York back then: the character of an area could run up and down scale within a matter of blocks. One could easily turn a corner in heaven and find oneself in hell.

CBGB was a pretty grungy place, spare and starkly furnished. The bathrooms were especially nasty, with walls covered in scabrous graffiti. It was all part of the punk lifestyle statement. The club had originally placed its stage in a peculiar location, scarcely twenty feet from the door and across from the bar. I was pleased to see that they had moved the stage to the back in shotgun shack formation. During T*he Breakfast Club* set,

Madonna was primarily playing the drums, but singing a few of her songs as well. She seemed slightly uncomfortable in front of the microphone and made up for her uneasiness by belching loudly mid song.

Angie Smit's bass playing had improved slightly, but not by much. She was making up for her mediocre musicianship by wearing lingerie on stage, which diverted attention from what Madonna felt was the group's main attraction, her. There was a guy with a blue Mohawk hairdo standing to the left of the stage making catcalls and wolf whistles at Angie, and Madonna was giving him the evil eye. It was a decent set of music, but one didn't get the feeling that anything earth shattering was taking place.

When Madonna came off stage, she was surly and annoyed. She was snapping at nearly everyone who attempted to speak to her. She didn't seem happy with the way the show had gone. I kept my distance, not wanting to be a target for her anger. She cornered me at the bar, asking me what I thought about the show.

"Well... You didn't seem very happy to be on stage."

"Yeah," she said. "I wanted to sing more, but I don't think Eddie likes my songs. It's a constant struggle with those two brothers deciding who gets the microphone."

"I can see how that could be frustrating."

Just then, the guy with the blue Mohawk walked up to Madonna, drunkenly singing the Jermaine Jackson song, "Let's Get Serious."

"Let's not and say we did, asshole!" she replied, giving him the brush-off.

It was clear from that night's performance that *The Breakfast Club* had a peculiar dynamic, like that of a two- headed horse running in opposite directions. It seemed like they could not carry on this way much longer

After several months of tension between the two sirens, Angie was let go. Dan and Eddie's original bassist, Gary

Burke moved back to New York and stepped in to fill the slot. The original Gilroy brother's band lineup was complete when original member Mike Monahan returned to play drums. Madonna continued to lobby for more time as lead singer. With Mike keeping a steady beat on the skins, she, Dan and Eddie were now sharing the vocal spotlight. Something had to give.

CHAPTER FOURTEEN
BO'S SPACE

I was still performing as lead singer for my group, *Steel Breeze*. Danny and I arranged to share a double bill for our respective bands, playing at a midtown loft venue called *Bo's Space*. It was not much of a spot, but it was spacious and we spent a good deal of effort preparing the interior, making it more presentable. We had the advantage of overseeing the entire event and extending the show as late as we wanted to, with festivities afterward well into the night. After the traditional coin toss, *Steel Breeze* won the coveted closing spot. This was a mixed blessing, as I knew that we would have to follow Madonna. I was confident that we could deliver a good set, but my heart was not entirely in it.

The Breakfast Club began setting up their equipment and as Mike loaded his drums onto the riser, Madonna stood off to the side. I walked over to her, my guitar slung over my shoulder.

"Have some of my coffee," I offered. "It's spiked with Kahlua." As she accepted the cup, I began to softly strum my guitar. "Let me play you a song I wrote for you. It's called 'My Little Angel.'"

It was a sappy song, overly romantic and trite, but I played it with conviction.

"I know you feel that you must leave.
There'd be no point for me to grieve.
When you were mine, you woke my heart.
But now it's time for us to part.
For you've things that you must do
A master plan that will come true.

Your destiny it waits for you,
My Little Angel."

She listened attentively as I played. "That's beautiful. It sounds like that guy David Gates from the group *Bread*."

"You bring out the romantic in me," I said.

I reached out to her and gently pulled her towards me, my hands around her waist, stroking her hips. She leaned forward, kissing my neck and nibbling my ear. I was swept away, completely forgetting my resolve to stay away from her while she was seeing Dan. I maneuvered her into an alcove in the shadows and we began to kiss.

Eddie called out, breaking the spell. "Let's Go! We're on in two minutes!"

Madonna pulled away and took a long hit of the spiked coffee. She then began working her body, stretching, loosening up, psyching herself. Then she turned to me smiling.
"We're gonna blow your group off the stage."

The Breakfast Club came out onstage all dressed in white, which perhaps was a bow to the current British New Romantic style. Madonna's hair was longer than I'd ever seen it and nicely styled in dark auburn waves. She started out playing an old Yamaha organ, pumping out a basic riff in the background while Danny sang lead. Next, Eddie sang a tune, while Madonna played his old Rickenbacker guitar, vamping like a she-Elvis.

Then she was on the mic, singing one of Danny's songs. *"Movin' along, Movin' along!" I just got to be on time. And here's what I'm hoping to find. I'm hoping to find with you. Love!"*

Suddenly she twisted, going down on one knee, and then she was snaking upward to the beat, moaning like a cat. I was mesmerized, really feeling the raw power of her stage presence for the first time. In that moment, the realization that Madonna would be a star and had always in fact been a star crystallized. The vague intuitive sense of her eventual success that I'd had was replaced by the absolute certainty that her fame would be monumental. That night I got the message that it was now Madonna's world and would remain so for quite some time.

When *The Breakfast Club's* set was over I walked over to congratulate Madonna, but several people had already surrounded her. Instead, I went over to Dan and Ed to tell them how much I enjoyed the show. I didn't mention that Madonna's stage presence had overshadowed them both and that I was concerned for the future of the band as an ensemble composed of equal members.

As *Steel Breeze* began setting up, our keyboard player, Kenee seemed to be having a problem with the Hammond organ that the Space's owner had loaned him. After ten minutes of Kenee vainly trying to get it going, Madonna, who had been watching us set up, walked over to see what the problem was.

"I can't get this ancient piece of crap to work!" said Kenee.

"Why don't you borrow mine?" Offered Madonna.

"Are you serious?" Kenee seemed pleasantly surprised and slightly overwhelmed by the generosity of the formerly distant siren. "That would be outstanding!" he said.

"Just make sure you get it back to me in one piece."

Our set was strong, but I sensed coldness in the audience reception. After *The Breakfast Club's* high-spirited antics, our music came off ponderous and self-important. Madonna later told me told this was not the sort of music she had expected from me.

"It's difficult to hear your voice over the guitars," she said. "Your bass player is too loud and he plays too much."

I was forced to agree.

Steel Breeze's manager, Gene, a heavy set, jovial Cuban walked over as we were talking.

"How'd you like to sing with *Steel Breeze?*" he asked Madonna.

"You must be joking!" she responded. "That music is definitely not my style. It sounds like something that my brother Martin used to listen to."

That was not the only offer Madonna received that night. Later in the evening, Madonna informed me that a rep from a small label called CoCo records had approached her, suggesting that she dump the band and go solo.

"No way am I gonna do that. Those guys are like my family," she said.

It was probably true for her in the moment, but I sensed that her feelings of loyalty and camaraderie would not last very long. It was abundantly clear to me that she was star material, and eventually the being inside her craving the spotlight would win out over the ensemble player. I was certain that this would not be the last time that someone would attempt to woo her away from her comrades in *The Breakfast Club*.

Weeks passed, and *The Breakfast Club* continued to rehearse, driven by Madonna's relentless perfectionism. She was a tireless promoter, constantly on the phone arranging gigs for the band. Her efforts to sing more of the material were paying off and she continued to write song after song, exploring her potential.

Madonna suddenly quit working for *Gossamer Wing*. She simply lacked the patience for such tedious labor, and she realized that her time could be better spent on promoting herself and the group. When Dan returned from work at the Wing, Madonna often had dinner ready for him. It was a fleeting moment of domestic bliss for him.

Madonna was becoming more confident in her ability to front a band. She was really paying attention to the more outspoken front women like *Blondie's* Deborah Harry and more crucially, *The Pretenders'* Chrissie Hynde. These women were part of a new breed of chanteuse with a sharper edge. Hynde in particular was cocky and cynical and played a mean guitar, a style that was more to Madonna's taste, as she assembled her own version of the "Kitten With a Whip." The more she performed, the more confident she became. She moved with the self-assurance of the dancer that she was, and used her entire body to accentuate what she was singing. Day by day, one could see more of what she was evolving into.

Gary and Mike were more and more in her corner, pressuring the Gilroys to make her the permanent lead singer. Dan and Eddie were not about to let this happen. In late summer of 1980, *The Breakfast Club* split up, The Gilroy brothers going one way and Madonna the other, taking Gary and Mike with her.

I called Dan a few days later to see how he was doing.

"I'm alright, Nar-man," Dan said. "You know I'm not the settling down kind."

"I know Bro, but you were pretty caught up in her."

"Yeah, but I'm a philosophical kind of guy. It was getting too stressful. It's all for the best."

"Sure Pal, whatever you say."

When I hung up the phone I couldn't stop myself from crying. I didn't know if it was for Dan or for myself.

Mike would soon quit when the pace and demands of rehearsal got too hectic. Madonna took this as an opportunity to phone her former Michigan boyfriend, Steve Bray, to step in as the new drummer. Bray arrived almost immediately, which was remarkably fortuitous for Madonna. Her power to conjure what she needed at a moment's notice remained formidable. Bray's precise sense of timing and musical ideas quickly brought the group to another level. When I called her on the phone one afternoon, she seemed preoccupied. I asked if I could see her sometime.

"I'm really busy with the new line-up," she said. "All I do is rehearse and make phone calls trying to hook shit up. Call me in a week or two. I'd like you to listen to what we've got."

"What are you calling yourselves?"

"It's either *Emmy* or *the Millionaires*."

Deep in the process of forging a new musical identity,

Madonna would be too preoccupied to socialize with me for several months.

CHAPTER FIFTEEN
THE MUSIC BUILDING

1980 came to a tragic conclusion. John Lennon's shocking death at the hand of a demented assassin seemed to put the final nail in the coffin that had been the 60s dream of harmony. I had lived just three blocks from *The Dakota*, the foreboding gothic structure that had been Lennon's home. On the night of December 8th I was on my way home when I saw the crowds surrounding the building. Having heard the devastating news, I walked back to my apartment in a daze. Like most children of my time, *The Beatles* had represented a breath of fresh air and a source of hope after the traumatic death of President Kennedy. Now, one of those heralds of youthful exuberance had been cut down in the same horrifying manner. It was as if again the heart and soul of a generation had been ripped out; leaving a wound that could never be completely healed. It was the wound of innocence irretrievably lost, and it was a harbinger of the changes in the decade to come. A harsh new world of technology and corporate materialism loomed in the future. "Greed is good" would become the phrase of the moment.

Strange to contemplate the fact that the freshness of punk music, partially a cynical response to what was perceived as the illusion of sixties idealism would eventually spawn new wave. That style, initially vital, would become increasingly more mechanized and bereft of soul, a perfect compliment to the reign of the computer just beginning to make inroads.

Sometime in early 1981, Madonna called, telling me to come have a look at her new lineup, at their rehearsal space in the infamous Music Building. They were calling the band *Emmy*, which was one of Madonna's old nicknames. *The Music Building* was just a block away from *Gossamer Wing*, on 8thAvenue near 38thStreet. That neighborhood was, and still is, one of the most chaotic spots on the planet. Nearby were the unsavory Port Authority Bus Terminal and the sleazy Times Square Porno district, converging with the bustling garment center. It was another classically grungy New York neighborhood. It was impossible not to feel like a serious dues-paying musician when one was working in such an environment. During the day, it was difficult to negotiate through the constant stream of auto and pedestrian traffic, exacerbated by aggressive young men pushing carts fully loaded with garments from warehouse to showroom. At night, ghoulish creatures skulked about the nearly abandoned dark and grimy streets in search of god-knows-what illicit pleasures.

The Music Building seemed skuzzy and run-down to me, but it had a certain funky charm. The eleven-story building was filled with seventy rehearsal studios, which were rented by the day or by the month. Visiting *The Music Building* made me feel that it was still possible for a band or a sound to grow from a grass roots level. The music business had not quite reached the stage where it completely controlled the direction of the music, and was capable of molding superstars like so many prefabricated TV dinners. MTV was just getting started, and there seemed to be a rush to find new acts to feed the machine. Madonna was coming up at just the right moment. As she crafted her look and her sound, Music Television was simultaneously developing the venue that would feature her in her best light. Up until the advent of Music Television, being a recording star did not necessarily require that one have an act with polished visual as well as musical presentation. As long as you sounded good, your records could be played regardless of your appearance. With the laser-keen eye of the video camera suddenly focused, a performer had to have a singular act, or at least a unique look. Madonna combined her distinctive sound with a quirky compelling fashion sense and an individual style of choreography, which put her in the same league as Michael Jackson, the only other MTV era performer with so complete a persona and a presentation package.

This of course would take several years to manifest. In 1981, Madonna was still living like a gypsy and grasping at musical stylistic straws to craft a garment that would fit her. The eclectic weirdness of *The Music Building* would provide several pieces of the puzzle gradually being assembled, and the grungy atmosphere of the place was perfect for the moment. The monstrous gentrification and commercial appropriation of everything was still a few years off. After 1980, when Ronald Reagan became president, everything would change forever. Even the hardcore sleaziness of Times Square would morph into a twisted version of nouveau Vegas Disneyland, like a theme park scale model of New York. A reign of corporate world domination would begin in earnest and Madonna's self styled Material Girl incarnation would have her moment in the sun.

I liked what I saw of *Emmy*. Steve Bray's drumming and production skills would be an asset to Madonna. Bray was African American, and the music that he co-authored and arranged was more R&B flavored. One of the tunes that they were fleshing out that night was "Everybody" which would become part of a demo that will eventually get the attention of Seymour Stein of Sire records. Madonna's new style reminded me of white R&B singer Teena Marie, who had worked with funk superstar Rick James. Madonna was sounding decidedly blacker than before, and it was a surprise to me, as I'd grown used to her as a punk. In fact, Madonna was returning to her *Motown* roots, reawakening the funk child that she had grown up as.

It made perfect sense. After all, Black dance moves embodied by someone like Michael Jackson were exploding on the scene, and the raw sexuality of the energy was powerfully compelling to Madonna's salacious nature. Black and Latin dance music was so much more lubricious than the comparatively bland synthesizer sounds of white pop. At its most intense, dance music was, in the words of Camille Paglia, "A grand Dionysian music with roots in African earth-cult."

I asked her where she was living, and she replied, "Here." Thinking that she was putting me on, I asked again and she reaffirmed that she was spending most nights in the studio. I feared for her life, as I could not imagine that this was possible. As street smart as she might be, it felt like this surreal neighborhood was too menacing even for her.

"Do you want go out after the rehearsal?" I asked.

"Well, I've kinda got a thing going on with Steve," She replied. "I'll call you next week and maybe we'll hang out together."

I didn't hear from her and chose not to pursue the matter. Whatever heat we'd had was on the wane. The fact was that I was no longer in her immediate orbit, a circle that was gradually becoming more exclusive.

Early in 1981, I went to see *Emmy* perform at my old alma mater, *Max's Kansas City*. The bar had lost nearly all of its hipness as far as I was concerned. It was no longer the hang out spot for the with-it underground, but it evoked memories. Madonna really poured it on for the Max's show, leaping onto tables and working the crowd like a lion tamer. Afterwards, from across the room, I saw a short haired, tough looking woman bring Madonna a cup of tea. They exchanged a few words and then Madonna threw her arms around the woman enthusiastically. Later, I learned that the woman was Camille Barbone, who owned a recording studio in *The Music Building*. Barbone had just offered Madonna a recording contract with her independent label, *Gotham Records*, which Madonna signed several days later.

I called Madonna about a week later. She told me that she was living in my favorite neighborhood, on Riverside

Drive, and that Camille had persuaded her to ditch the band, abandon her guitar and focus on her dancing skills to augment her singing. I told her that that made perfect sense to me, as she was a dancer to begin with. I asked her if she wanted to go for a stroll in the park and she replied that she was much too busy with rehearsals. I wished her the best and this was the last time that I spoke to her.

Several weeks later, I was amused to hear from Dan Gilroy that Madonna would be performing on New Year's Eve at a club called *My Father's Place*, opening for *The New York Dolls*, the Godfathers of Punk. I decided not to go to the show. It felt to me as if I was senselessly pursuing her, and to no avail. She was generally warm to me, but I sensed that I was not likely to ever be intimate with her again. The only available option was for me be a part of her charmed inner circle, and that position had no appeal to me.

Then, out on the town in *Danceteria*, I saw Madonna with her posse, Erika Bell, Debi Mazar and several others. She knew that I was there, but she was ignoring me more or less. She was enjoying another "Buzzbomb" moment, dancing wildly with a crowd surrounding her. I sat at a table with Erika and had a drink. I watched Madonna and another girl dancing with a guy and suddenly they began humping him, yelling, *Webo, Webo!*
I asked Erika what this Webo shit was about.

"We're turning the tables on the Spanish boys," she replied. Webo means Ballsy, and the boys that hump girls on the dance floor call it the Webo dance, so we do it to them back."

I was seriously annoyed that Madonna had dissed me at *Danceteria*. She seemed to be moving further away from nearly everyone she had known prior to her new success. This feeling was confirmed when I spoke to a girl who had known Madonna from the time she had worked at *Gossamer Wing*. Like Curtis Zale, Lisa had been one of Madonna's most ardent supporters from the beginning, attending nearly all of her gigs. Lisa told me that both she and Curtis had been calling Madonna regularly, keeping track of her performance schedule so that they could support her. Apparently, Madonna had suddenly changed her number without informing them, or for that matter, me. The girl was enjoying her newfound power and starting to draw her inner circle in tighter around her. That power was beginning to have its sway over her and she was changing. It mattered little to me, as I had little inclination to consort with celebrities in order to make my life complete. The only regret I had was that I had lost a friend whom I had believed that I had a connection with.

In September 1981, I moved to Los Angeles for nearly a year. I got a job singing standards and early rock n' roll in a piano bar, and I focused on my singing. I hung out at Venice Beach and spent a lot of time working out in the outdoor weightlifters pen. The sport of bodybuilding and an obsession with physical culture was just beginning to mushroom into a worldwide cult. It occurred to me that something that I started doing six years earlier, which at the time was looked upon as a peculiar aberration and sub-culture, was becoming increasingly more main stream. What I did not realize was that weight training would grow even more prevalent, becoming the regimen of nearly every competitive sport, even including the workouts of Madonna and her ilk.

When I returned to New York, I took up with a girl named Ellen, who was the daughter of Sidney Kaye, owner of *The Russian Tea Room*. She was a great torch singer, and we spent our weekends singing and drinking Jack Daniels at a Bleecker Street bar called *The Surf Maid* with a cool pianist named Claude Garvey. I decided to forget about pop music and pursuing the fleeting dream of rock stardom.

What I did not witness over that year was a period of time that was critical to Madonna's success and emergence as an original and bona fide superstar. Flush with her moderate success, Madonna proceeded to immerse herself in the downtown scene, luxuriating in the underground. With her gang of sexually aggressive *Webo* girls in tow, she absorbed essences from all aspects of the local New York scene, from Bronx break dancing, hip-hop and graffiti to Latin and Salsa flavored music, dance and fashion, to punk and new wave rock. She then mixed it up with New Romantic styles of dress and make-up and her own blend of *Motown* wildness.

Madonna became a regular at *Danceteria*, getting close to deejay Mark Kamins. One the hippest clubs around at the time, the West Twenty-first Street venue attracted a regular crowd of partygoers who were in the know as far as what was cutting edge. Kamins, another New York native with his finger on the pulse would quickly notice the charismatic singer/dancer making moves on the floor while surrounded by her posse of acolytes.

Like me and others before me, the deejay could spot Madonna's star power and was happy to spin her track "Everybody" which she had produced with Steve Bray. The club's crowd responded enthusiastically, and based on that positive reaction, Kamins brought Madonna's demo to Seymour Stein, hooking her up with the label where she has remained since that day. The city itself was clearly conspiring to propel the Mid-western girl to the heights of fame.

Then too, she became a regular at Andy Warhol's Factory, taking up with graffiti and fine artist Jean Michel Basquiat. In the presence of master media manipulator Warhol, she obviously learned a thing or two about promotion. Time spent in a professional and romantic relationship with Bronx native DJ and producer, "Jellybean" Benitez was also a plus in her development and education. Having abandoned her guitar, Madonna was devoid of props. Now, she had to rely on her body, her style and her voice alone to present herself. Without external instruments, her body became her instrument, and how she projected it took on even greater importance than her voice.

As silly as it may sound, *Webo* was a key element there, a major factor in her philosophy and way of confronting the world. More and more in her performance, Madonna emphasized the aggressive sexual dominatrix inside herself. She began performing with other dancers that supported and magnified her. She took charge of the choreography and injected all of the influences that she had absorbed into her individual stylistic mix. Her stage persona solidified as she interacted with her dancers, many of whom were gay men whose stage roles accentuated their passivity. On stage, Madonna became the Queen Bitch and they were her slaves. In essence, this was an extension of that part of herself that had always played the sexual aggressor and had insisted that she was the one in charge. Madonna would never allow herself to be manipulated by Svengali-like media moguls. If she was anyone's victim, it would only be of her own compulsive impulse to provoke.

For the first time, all these disparate and eclectic elements coalesced into a cohesive package, a unique personality never before witnessed. After years of experimentation with herself, she arrived in that period of early to mid 1982. Five years in New York had molded her into the perfect hybrid. She was the "Hothouse Flower" blossoming in the rare botanical garden of the city. Having grown up in a time that still had memories of old school Hollywood films, classical dance and music, she had carried the legacy of her childhood, including her middle class Catholic Midwestern self, to the crucible of modern high and low culture. Although it was not instantly apparent to most critics, Madonna blended the trashy street punk waif with the glamour and elegance of the Hollywood goddess. Like the city she dwelled in, Madonna straddled the line, exploring the extreme opposites of glitz and grit. When her "Boy Toy" image was ready, Madonna stormed Music Television. Prior to her appearance there, because of her dance-oriented sound, many listeners assumed that she was Black. When she appeared on the screen, her fate was sealed. The combination of her looks, her style, her moves and her sound was irresistible. Madonna instantly spawned the "Wannabes" a legion of girls who imitated her distinct look. When she was ready for her next transformation, the "Wannabes" would reincarnate as well.

Although it probably goes without saying, the advent of Music Television changed everything, irrevocably and forever. The development and presentation of an act, always somewhat dependent on image, now became image centric. Image trumped sound as the pre-eminent factor for success. Madonna, always Image conscious from the core of her being would be out of the gate and one step ahead from the get-go. From video to video, she would exhibit an uncanny sense of how to reinvent herself in order to give us a fresh iconic image. Madonna, with her eye on the Hollywood glamour of the past as her inspiration, would project those borrowed images into her future.

I was blissfully unaware of all of these developments. I thought little of Madonna during that spring until I heard that she had signed with Sire records. Her old roommate, Susan informed me that she was performing regularly doing club dance music. She had totally abandoned her former persona of New Wave rocker. Still, I didn't really know what to expect. When I heard that she was performing with her new act at *The Ritz*, a predominantly New Wave club near Union Square, I was overcome with curiosity. I realized that I had to go and see for myself precisely what she had become.

CHAPTER SIXTEEN
THE RITZ

The Ritz was a large renovated dance hall cum theater with a stage. It was the perfect performance venue as far as I was concerned, big enough for loud live music, but intimate enough so that one could get close enough to the performers. There were no seats, only the dance floor and the stage.

Backed up by two other dancers, Madonna gyrated and sang over a taped track. She performed a short set, a four-song sample from her first album.

It was the first time I was to see Madonna in the style of dress that she would adopt. She wore black fish net stockings and a short black dress, with a profusion of bracelets and necklaces. She also wore a crucifix to emphasize the religious iconic significance of her name, which she had now adopted without compromise or modification. Most surprisingly, she was now a blonde, or at least sporting blonde streaks in her naturally brown hair.

Her voice was strong and passionate with a plaintive quality, as she sang, "*I'm Burning Up, Burning up for your Love!*" The music was catchy pop, light and infectious. Every song had a repetitive hook in its chorus such as, "*Everybody, Come on Dance and Sing. Everybody, Get up and Do Your Thing.*" She had even knocked off Olivia Newton John, with a song that climaxed with a chorus of "*Physical attraction, Chemical reaction.*"

My immediate reaction was that they were almost like children's songs, but they were compelling. Even more, they were danceable.

Madonna had created a dance style for herself, which was deceptively simple, enabling her to have enough breath to sing, while she stayed in motion. She moved easily, stepping from side to side and punctuating the lyrics with hand gestures. Occasionally she would spin around and drop to the ground, but she nearly always maintained eye contact with someone in the audience. Her dancers, Erika Belle and a man that I didn't recognize mirrored her moves.

I could plainly see that the ambitious little street urchin girl had finally arrived at her destination, although I did not realize how far she had yet to go to reach her true ambition, to rule the world. I stood there, ten feet from the stage, hands on my hips, laughing with appreciation. The crowd wasn't large, but they were enthusiastic. They were impressed, as I was, by the syncopated moves that she and her dancers were performing, as well as by her overwhelming confidence.

In mid lyric, she noticed me standing just beyond the footlights. She smiled warmly and began to crank it up as if deriving vitality by my presence, focusing the full force of her energy on me. I was nailed to the wall, certain in that moment of what I had known intuitively all along: She was about to leave the mundane world behind and enter a world of her own making. I left the club without going backstage. I no longer felt that I was a part of her world.

MY MADONNA
AFTERWORD

I have not seen Madonna in person since that night at *The Ritz*. As I have watched her career unfold over the decades I find myself wondering if I ever truly knew who she was. The fact is, I never really got to know her beyond a certain point, and so my experience of her person is perpetually filtered through my own preconceptions.

Madonna's career has always been so much about the shifting images that she has taken on and discarded as a performer, that it is a fascinating study to contemplate them. One of the first images that Madonna adopted professionally was her impersonation of Marilyn Monroe in the *Material Girl* video. The short film was so potent that it instantly made people associate her with the tragic celluloid goddess, but it struck a sour note for me with its evocation of a gold-digging floozy.

The Madonna that I remember was a free spirit, something like her character in the film *Desperately Seeking Susan*. She was completely unpretentious, a sort of trickster goddess who could disarm and baffle all that was stuffy and self- important. But in reality, Madonna was desperately seeking fame, and fame is the great corruptor. Madonna's fame took her very far from the girl that I thought I knew.

In some sense, the 1985 film *Desperately Seeking Susan* was not only a major factor in Madonna's success but an encoded account of her transmutation from ordinary Midwestern girl to New York pop goddess. Roberta, Rosanna Arquette's character, is a bored and unfulfilled suburban housewife who goes across the GW Bridge to New York and becomes fixated on a charismatic bohemian girl named Susan, played by Madonna. Roberta follows Susan to an East Village boutique and buys the jacket that Susan has traded for a pair of jeweled boots. The jacket is decorated with a magical Masonic pyramid symbol like the one on the back of a dollar bill, and was rumored to have belonged to Jimi Hendrix (or Elvis). Inside the pocket of the jacket is a key to a locker containing Susan (Madonna's) possessions. Roberta is hit on the head while wearing the jacket and loses own her identity to become Susan.

Themes of magic and transformation inform the film. It is down the Rabbit Hole in the classic sense. New York functions as Oz, the Emerald City of Witchcraft. With its myriad locations full of mirth, menace and mayhem, it is as much a player in the farce as any of the characters are.

We first see Madonna (Susan) also leave New Jersey and enter a place called *The Magic Club,* where Roberta goes later in search of her identity.

Roberta ends up working at *The Magic Club* as a magician's assistant. Susan contacts Roberta's befuddled husband to learn the lost girl's whereabouts. They meet in an underground disco, giving us a taste of the New York bohemian music scene that Madonna has just risen from in real life. The scene is doubly powerful as it is Madonna's song *"Get Into the Groove"* that is playing on the dance floor as Susan questions the husband. In a subliminal cameo, we also see a partygoer in the background wearing a Marilyn Monroe T-shirt.

Madonna's character is a trickster archetype, whose antics allow the other players to become who they truly are. She is a sort of *Scaramouche,* who with her streetwise canniness, appears to be giving sly asides to the audience who are in on her jokes.

In the end, the role reversal is complete, ironically because the film, which was conceived as a star vehicle for Arquette became the breakout role in which Madonna came into her own. She emerges as the hippest character in the film, in a brilliant star turn that could not possibly have been more spot-on for her essential nature in that moment in time.

That character, the worldly gamine with street smarts and sex appeal to spare is the one that her "Wannabes" wanted to become, as Arquette did in the film when she donned the magic jacket.

Clearly, Madonna is no longer that person. The degree of fame that she has attained no longer permits her the luxury of being a fairly anonymous spirit of the streets of New York, freely spreading mischief and enlightenment. Be that as it may, Madonna still functions as a trickster. She tweaks convention on a much larger playing field, where she can shake up the entire world instead of merely the neighborhood.

Strangely, or perhaps not so, that girl from 1979 still visits me in dreams, where we cavort in the city street as we did so long ago, so in a certain sense, my Madonna, like the character in the film still exists.

Madonna the trickster continued to push buttons as her career progressed. In 1992, she released a coffee table book called *Sex*, which purported to reveal Madonna's range of erotic fantasies. What struck me most about the book was the degree that she incorporated fairly conventional images of bondage and fetishism, as if she were trying to reach out and shock a certain sector of society. Knowing what I did of Madonna's sexuality, the book did not ring true. It felt like an attempt to capitalize on other people's fantasies of what she was. Even author Camille Paglia, touted as the anti-feminist feminist, who championed Madonna as a bold new role model for sexually liberated women stated in so many words that she was disappointed in the crassness of Madonna's approach to *Sex*.

My own sexual experience of Madonna was that she was deeply and profoundly a sensualist, something that was missing in all the leather bondage imagery in the Sex book. When Madonna was using sexual artifice, it would always seem insincere to me. This would occur in movie roles and videos that felt staged and unnatural. It would also appear in social situations when she would put on a sexually provocative facade. It was only when she was comfortable with someone or with herself that her natural sensuality would flow effortlessly.

Also conspicuously absent from the book was much in the way of romanticism. Madonna's inner lover responded and surrendered most completely to the sea of passion in which she could be completely swept away. This was not my experience of her alone. Other people who had gotten close to Madonna found themselves surprised by her proclivity towards tenderness.

Without that element of romance there is little left in sex but an exchange of body fluids. Perhaps it was again the fear of surrendering to what felt like an overwhelming world of emotion that drove Madonna away from an exploration of the center and closer to the impersonal surface imagery of sex. Although the book sold well due to its sensational nature, in the end it felt like a mis-step. Still, after all, it did not seem to do Madonna's career any harm and succeeded in the obvious way of bringing her publicity.

As usual, I found myself consistently surprised at the relentless advance of Madonna's career. I continued to monitor her progress, laughing approvingly or shaking my head in dismay.

I've often considered writing a memoir such as this, but have never before been able to collect my thoughts in a way that satisfied me. Perhaps I have been reluctant to write about Madonna because my memories of her felt like a private matter and not an appropriate topic for prurient small talk. Over the years I have often dreamed about her, and in those dreams, she appears not so much as a lover, but as a friend, a companion with whom I often find myself walking the streets of New York as we did in the past. In those dreams, she again seems more like an elemental spirit than a person that I want or need anything from. Maybe that is why I sometimes entertain the idea that the person that I knew was a fabrication of my imagination, like one of the muses. What is certain is that Madonna was and is a changeling, a person capable of absorbing essences and moving on to something new. Perhaps that is why her persona is often so difficult to pin down.

Over the years, I have read various accounts of Madonna's life, and I can see that each author has their own perspective and bends the facts to fit this particular spin. In this respect I am probably no different, although my intent is not to sensationalize any aspect of her life.

The first biography of Madonna that I am aware of was called *Lucky Star*. It was written by Michael McKenzie and appeared in 1985, just after Madonna's career started taking off in earnest. Much of the author's information on her start in the music business came from an interview with Dan Gilroy. It was Danny, my old friend who named me as the guy that brought the two of them together and it was probably his description of me that the author used: "Burroughs was a cross between Burt Reynolds and Batman."

Personally, I would have preferred being described as a cross between Marlon Brando and the Silver Surfer.

I have been interviewed several times for various Madonna biographies, and I have been consistently amazed by how often what is said to a journalist comes out differently in print. It's sort of like that party game "telephone" when you whisper something to someone in a circle and wait for it to come around again to see how badly, or hilariously, it has been corrupted.

In 1992, I was interviewed for a biography called *The Madonna Scrapbook*, by Lee Randall, and I was given a special interview section where I was quoted directly. Just prior to the interview I'd been studying mythology, which is one of my interests. I read that the Roman goddess Diana, also called Artemis by the Greeks, had a festival that was celebrated on

August 13th. I found that quite intriguing, as I knew that
Madonna's birthday was August 16th. I read on. Diana was the
goddess of the hunt and of the moon as well as of the hearth.
She was also a protector of virgins and women in labor, and
she carried a torch in her right hand. She is also considered to
be a pagan version of the Christian Madonna.

I couldn't help but think of Madonna as a modern
incarnation of Diana/Artemis. I made mention of this
connection in my interview for *The Madonna Scrapbook*, and it
was printed more or less verbatim. Then in 2000, biographer
Barbara Victor interviewed me for a Madonna biography that
would eventually be called *Goddess*. She used my observation
that Madonna was a modern incarnation of Diana/Artemis
as the central theme of her book. So, am I now responsible
for the perpetuation of the idea that Madonna is a Goddess?
What will be the repercussions of this? Elvis Presley, dead for
almost thirty-five years is worshipped as a saint, and people visit
Graceland to be miraculously cured of their afflictions. What
does the future hold for a woman who is already considered a
goddess?

Fame is a very strange condition. As a teenager, I developed
a strong craving for it that lasted well into adulthood. Much
of what fascinated me had been the murky reasons why some
people came to prominence, while others remained obscure.
What was the secret ingredient? I also wondered why some
people seemed capable of handling fame's pressures, whereas
those same pressures were capable of destroying others.

As a young man, I had the opportunity to study this
phenomenon more intimately when I saw this woman whom
I had known and loved, anointed with fame practically before
my eyes. From afar, I carefully observed how she had adapted to
its pressures and constraints. I felt as if I had been close enough
to the flame to get burned. Because of Dan's testimony, my
life had been inextricably intertwined with Madonna's in the
public eye. I began to notice that people would often treat me

differently when they knew that I had been touched by one of the Olympians. Did I really need to get any closer to the maelstrom?

People who I hadn't heard from in years would call me out of the blue, having just seen me in a TV interview. One such friend retorted crassly, "You always wanted to be the next Elvis, but instead you ended up fucking her."

My brief opportunity to experience anything remotely resembling fame came in the unexpected form of a House music group called *Kraze*. The group was born in the Brooklyn basement of front man Richard Laurent. Rich's two sisters Martine and Mirielle were backup singers, and I also sang and played guitar. We also used various keyboard and percussive instruments, which set us apart from most House Music acts who usually sang over a pre-recorded track. I began performing with them in the summer of 1986, after meeting Richard when I hired him to work in an air brush t-shirt company that I was managing.

House Music was underground dance music played late at night. It basically started at the *Warehouse Club* in Chicago, where a DJ named Frankie Knuckles began mixing different tracks together and adjusting the beats to about 125 beats per minute. As a result, the music never had to stop or the tempo slow down. The persistent throb of the bass put revelers into a kind of hypnotic trance. Another important house music club was New York's own *Paradise Garage,* whose DJ was Larry Lavan, a cutting edge star of the turntable.

During the 1980s, the Paradise Garage had been arguably one of the most influential clubs in the world. Madonna was a regular Garage performer in her early days, also filming the video for her first hit "*Everybody*" there. The patrons were for the most part well-heeled gay men in the fashion and entertainment industry, who worked hard during the day and partied like demons far into the night. Next to Chicago's Frankie Knuckles, Larry Lavan was the other DJ most responsible for the House Music phenomenon. Levan mixed music on three turntables, segueing in and out of different records while syncopating the Beats per minute to keep the groove going.

Levan was a champion of *Kraze's* unique species of house music, eventually enabling us to tour Europe. In America, House Music never made it out of the underground. It was a shadowy, twilight world, inhabited by beings that faded away like ghosts when the sun came up. In our own town, we were anonymous, but in Europe it was quite a different story. What *Kraze* had started in a Brooklyn basement created waves overseas that doubled back to America and even had an effect on my old friend Madonna.

The release of *Kraze's* record "*The Party*" created an instant buzz in the New York House Music scene. Although it was not played much on the local radio, House music had a huge following on the dance music charts. It was an enormous sub culture that few people were even aware of. One of the clubs we performed in, *The World*, was a large auditorium dance hall on the Lower East Side that I later found out was one of Madonna's favorite hangouts. One night, *Kraze* visited *The World* at 2:00 A.M. to sign some records for the D.J. Madonna had apparently been there for several hours, but she had just left a few minutes earlier. Completely out of touch with her world, I hadn't even realized that she was exploring mine.

I began thinking about her again, fantasizing. What would it be like to see Madonna again? Had she heard about me? Would she even care? It seemed as if I was on my way to something bigger. Would that matter to her? I thought again about fame. How had she changed? Would I be able to relate to her? Several friends suggested that I attempt to contact her, but I didn't feel comfortable with the idea. What if she didn't respond? My pride told me to wait: If I was meant to see her again then I would. I would leave it in the hands of the gods.

By the autumn of 1988, *Kraze* had set up a two-week tour

of Italy, where our record, "The Party" was quickly climbing the pop music charts. From there, it was on to France in the early spring of 1989. Stationed in Paris, we traveled by car or train, playing shows in cities throughout the country. It was quickly decided that I was the member of the band to give interviews, because I was reasonably well spoken and could collect my thoughts under the pressure of the media. I was therefore asked all sorts of questions about *Kraze*, what we symbolized and what our intentions were. At some point, I had let it be known among the group that I had once dated Madonna. Our manager, Craig Kallman began working this fact into press releases, and soon I was answering interviewer's questions about my relationship with her. I generally wouldn't make too much of the matter, acknowledging that it was true and then trying to change the subject. Often, I was asked if I'd seen her lately, to which I'd reply, "I don't think she knows I'm alive."

Then, during a promotional appearance at a record store on the outskirts of Paris, a DJ approached me.

"Madonna was in here a few weeks ago, looking for some new sounds. She saw your photograph on the *Kraze* record. She said, 'I know this guy.'"

Madonna, with her finger on the pulse and her ear to the ground, scouting out new styles for herself, had found something fresh. House music, with its hypnotic sub-bass bottom and compulsive beat that kept time with the racing human heart was a perfect direction for her to explore. The music was flowing into a direction that recalled the sixties in its pursuit of hedonism and ecstatic pleasure. As a matter of fact, the drug of choice among house music fanciers was a mild hallucinogen called Ecstasy. It had the effect of lowering inhibitions and heightening sensory pleasure, encouraging freer sexuality, but it also fostered a sort of empathetic euphoria among those gathered in celebration. It was the ultimate mood altering party drug.

All of this would have appealed to Madonna, not only because of the sexual aspect, but also because of the sense of a communal movement that surrounds the music. Again, this phenomenon was so much more apparent in Europe than in America. In England, Prime Minister Margaret Thatcher had briefly considered the idea of banning house music from the BBC, because she felt that it was contributing to an escalating drug problem.

Traveling overseas regularly, Madonna had clearly seen what was a burgeoning musical force in the European world. It was something that seemed to be gaining a strong, if somewhat less potent foothold in the New York scene, and Madonna wanted in on it.

Years later, when interviewed for a documentary, legendary House pioneer DJ Frankie Knuckles stated that he knew that House music had gone mainstream when he heard Madonna's track, "*Vogue*."

Well, that might be an overstatement. Whatever elements of House music went into "*Vogue*" were quickly absorbed and barely noticed by the general music consuming population. House, Trance, Techno: who indeed could tell the difference? Therein lay the problem. In America, House was too amorphous a style to properly identify, and the aspects of it that could be identified often posed a threat. In Europe, the audience for house was varied, coming from several demographics, races and lifestyles. House music was played on pop radio stations regularly. It was popular precisely because it had come from the American underground.

In America, House enthusiasts were generally Gay or Black. That's why the style was perfect for the camp vamping of Madonna's "*Vogue*." It gave Middle-America a taste of forbidden fruit, of a lifestyle that was strange and exotic, presented by someone safe and familiar enough to encompass it. Madonna worked with cutting edge producer Shep Pettibone, using the piano vamp intro, the sub bass and the 125 beat per minute tempo of House to make a hit record, and then moved on as she was wont to do.

Still, I am proud that Madonna, however briefly embraced House Music, because as far as I am concerned, "*Vogue*" is the penultimate Madonna record. "*Vogue*" is the pinnacle of her career and a personal statement that embodies nearly all that she stands for or has made of herself. Madonna was celebrating old school glamour: the stars that she mentions in the song are from her childhood and from a time when a star was an enduring legend. "*Vogue*" is a testament to the belief that striking a pose is everything. It is the certitude that you can create and if need be, re-create yourself again and again.

As a music video, "*Vogue*" also perfectly sums up and encapsulates Madonna's association with Music videos. From MTV's inception, Madonna has been one of the people that have truly shaped its direction, and with her relentless change of personas she has always striven to strike a pose and assume the character in the mode that "Vogue" suggests.

Although she has struggled somewhat in her film career, Madonna's status as an icon of visual media is secure, because she has created a persona in Music video as enduring as that of any film star. Her best movie roles are those that reinforce that character. Throughout the span of her career, the tough but tender gamine that Madonna portrayed in *Desperately Seeking Susan* gradually mated with the Monroe-esque glamour girl from the Material Girl video to produce Dick Tracy's gangster moll nemesis Breathless Mahoney. That character is a manifestation of the exquisite being that Madonna presents to us in Vogue. It is a complete portrait of a celluloid creature as striking and remote as Garbo or Dietrich, as alluring and sexually potent as Monroe and as tough as Harlow, Mae West or Bette Davis.

Of course, the most iconic film role Madonna has tackled would certainly have to be that of *Evita*. In the mid 90's at a point when her star was somewhat on the wane, Madonna would hunger for the role that would put her back on top. What could be more appealing to a self described control freak, whose stated goal was to rule the world than the rags to riches story of a woman who married a politician and due to her glamour and charisma became a populist national saint.

As a musical, the film plays like a prolonged music video of which Madonna is the star in her ascendancy. Surrounded by adoring crowds, she basks in their admiration. People worship her image as a religious icon and chant her name like a mantra. Madonna won a golden globe for her performance. Even more appropriate to the size of her ego, the Academy award winning song that she closed the film with was entitled, "You Must Love Me."

Sometime in the mid-summer of 1992, I got a strange phone call from someone who said that he was "Slam," or Oliver. When I appeared confused as to his identity, he told me that he was one of the dancers on Madonna's *Blonde Ambition* tour. As a secondary credential he mentioned his role in the film *Truth or Dare*. I asked him which dancer he was, and he said, "I'm black, with blonde hair."

Oliver said that he was calling to invite me to Madonna's birthday party, which was to be held in Los Angeles or perhaps Miami. "I didn't think that she would remember me," I said. "Oh, she remembers you."

Thinking that this might be some sort of hoax, I told him that I'd be delighted to come, but couldn't spare the airfare. If someone would send me a round trip ticket, I ventured, I would be there for sure. Oliver said that he would see what he could do. I never heard from him again. It was a peculiar moment, which to this day I can make little sense of. It was an exciting prospect, but certainly the stuff that dreams were made of. Was I being summoned by the inner circle, the subject of a practical joke or at the mercy of the fantasies of a young man? I'll probably never know.

The film, *Truth or Dare* was to me one of the most surreal moments of Madonna's career for various reasons, primarily because it pretended to be a documentary, but was in reality a way for the star to exploit the most intimate relationships and aspects of her life. Watching the film really reinforced my previously noted sensation that nearly all the people in Madonna's life were literally or figuratively co-stars in her movie. Having lived in the spotlight since she was in her mid-twenties, Madonna has literally grown from a girl to a woman on camera, and her trials and tribulations and those of the people closest to her, including her family are worked out in front of an audience of millions.

Watching the portion of the film featuring Madonna's then bosom buddy Sandra Bernhard, I thought about the fact that I had met the comedienne long ago in 1976, on a blind date in Los Angeles, which had to have been one of the strangest moments of my life and one of the greatest mismatches of personality I've ever experienced. I had briefly moved to L.A. on a whim, and a New York friend with some Hollywood connections gave me Bernhard's phone number and suggested that I ring her up. We met for lunch one afternoon and sat across from each other with virtually nothing to say. When I discovered that Sandra Bernhard and Madonna had become friends it was one of the great "What the Fuck?" moments in recent memory.

The comedienne's peculiar Puckish ways brought out even more of the trickster in Madonna, and the duo seemed to exult in a plethora of elaborate mind games and put-ons that were to me more baffling than amusing. But there was more to it than just mere companionship, despite the trappings of lesbianism that came with the affair.

Madonna's relationship with Bernhard seemed to fulfill a particular void in the star's life when she appeared to be having trouble trusting anyone. Bernhard's powerfully cynical and acerbic personality was clearly what Madonna needed during her traumatic breakup with her first husband, Sean Penn. As was her wont, when that need no longer existed, Madonna severed the relationship with Bernhard, who responded by saying, "We don't speak anymore. I keep my friends my whole life, but Madonna feels differently." Not an uncommon sentiment among people who have spent time with the ethereal material girl.

Over the years, I remained in contact with several of Madonna's old band mates. In particular, I stayed in touch with Dan Gilroy who has remained my friend to this day. Sometime around 1984, Dan and Ed teamed up with Steve Bray and Gary Burke in a more successful version of *The Breakfast Club*, releasing a track in 1987 called "Right on Track" that went to number seven on the U.S. charts. The group also recorded a version of *The Beatles*' song, "Drive My Car", which appeared in the comedic film, *License To Drive*.

Bray of course went on to work with Madonna again, writing and producing several tracks with her.

It seemed however that Madonna was someone who seldom looked back on her roots, to validate those that had given her a hand or a leg up. That's why I was astounded when I heard her speech in 2008, when Madonna was inducted into *The Rock and Roll Hall of Fame*. Her words were a touching and emotionally revealing foray into the genesis of her career. In it, she acknowledged the incredible chain of fortuitous events that had brought her to that moment on stage.

"I have always been fortunate to have people around me who believed in me," she said. After acknowledging her Ballet teacher back in Michigan, Madonna continued.

"And then there was Dan Gilroy. He lived in an abandoned synagogue in Queens with his brother Ed. They played in a band together. I was sick of being an out of work dancer, so he taught me how to play guitar.

"There's a saying in the Talmud, that for every blade of

grass there's an angel that watches over it, and whispers, Grow, Grow, and I can still hear those whispers."

What finally prompted to write about my experiences with Madonna was discovering that her daughter Lourdes had enrolled in the *LaGuardia High School of the Arts* in New York's Lincoln Center. The school was a merger of my old high school, *Music and Art* and the *School of Performing Arts*, featured prominently in the movie *Fame*. Although she had been born in Los Angeles and had lived in England as well, little Lola was settling into New York as a stable home. It certainly seemed like the logical place for Madonna's child to be educated.
I had the sudden realization of the degree that the city itself had been complicit in Madonna's rise to stardom.

Madonna had come to New York a lost soul, searching for a way to make a mark on the world. Almost immediately, without a single reservation, the town had taken her in and sustained her, like a magical womb of gestation. Almost as soon as she had stepped of the Greyhound bus, with literally no place to go, a Good Samaritan had taken her into his Manhattan Plaza-off Times Square home.

She was instantly accepted to study with Pearl Lang and as soon as she was ready to abandon formal dance training, she re-connected with me and found Dan Gilroy to begin her musical education in a Corona synagogue. When it was time to leave the security of that space, she found Camille Barbone and then Mark Kamins and the club-land atmosphere of *Danceteria* to nourish her.

Like Roberta in *Desperately seeking Susan*, Madonna had been transformed magically as soon as she set foot in New York City. True, her adopted hometown was an often-painful crucible for the forging of Madonna's abilities. Overnight success was actually made up of years of blind struggle, but throughout the journey, another door had mysteriously opened as soon as one had closed. If there was an angel watching over

Madonna's metaphorical growing blade of grass, it was most certainly a native New York angel.

As Madonna has just released a new record and is on tour as I write this, one has to wonder what it is she is hoping to accomplish for the remainder of her life. Is it simply the desire to remain relevant and in the spotlight? Madonna has admitted to being an adrenaline junkie, addicted to excitement, but there appears to be more going on than meets the eye. Madonna has spoken extensively about her quest for art that will transform the world. This sort of thinking is not that uncommon among performers, but one has to wonder just how realistic and feasible that ambition actually is. Clearly, Madonna has already changed the world by having displayed her outsize personality for the past thirty odd years, but is there more that she can do?

There is a strong spiritual craving at work inside her that borders on a messiah complex, but this sort of mass spiritual transformation thing has rarely been done musically, with the exception of groups like *The Beatles*, who were part of a larger spiritual zeitgeist which is totally lacking today.

Madonna has attempted to effect spiritual changes using music with her 1998 album, *Ray of Light*. It is an astonishing piece of work that in my mind certainly should have had at least some subtle impact on human consciousness if the world had been appropriately receptive to it. That is the essential secret of the universe. Timing is everything. In order for someone to change the world, the world itself must be prepared for the transformation.

Madonna's persona is so outsized that she practically must do something astoundingly radical in order to transcend it. I for one have no idea of what that could be, because she has already ventured further than most entertainers could ever dream of.

Of course what she will most likely do is try to retain her Queen of Pop crown by trying to out-rock the competition. This will probably work on some level, but that almost certainly will not be enough to satisfy her for very long. According to her previous track record, she will then be looking around for what to accomplish next. She must realize that she cannot realistically retain control over a market designed for consuming youth and vitality, even though many of her successors are pale shadows of what Madonna was in her prime.

Madonna's own shadow is so large that those who have lived within it are transformed inexorably. On reflection, another thing that prompted me to write this book was a belief that by doing so, I might possibly come to terms with the reality that a portion of my identity is intertwined with Madonna's. For example, several years ago, I took up a Yoga practice and shortly thereafter discovered coincidentally that my instructor/masseur Leslie also occasionally did bodywork on Madonna. Having received a massage one afternoon, I emerged into the anteroom to discover actress Gwyneth Paltrow waiting for her appointment. Paltrow was currently in Madonna's circle of friends. Without missing a beat, Leslie introduced us.

"Gwyneth," he said. "This is Norris, an old friend of Madonna's."

I smiled and took her hand. After all, I was not just Norris Nobody. I was Madonna's friend and therefore rated an introduction.

As I write, Madonna is of course in the process of re-inventing herself yet again. The elemental spirit that I recognized so long ago has proven to be durable enough to sustain a thirty-year career. She has indeed shown me, and the world, a great deal about the nature of fame. There are legions of celebrities who have had a run in the spotlight less than half as long as Madonna's, before burning out or fading away. Although she is perhaps past her prime, Madonna shows little sign of doing either. She is the mother of several children, who undoubtedly have changed her perspective on the world. She appears to have become a kinder, gentler Madonna, more centered and at peace with herself. She has become a Yogini and embraced Kabbalah, which is ironically appropriate for someone who took on her musical education in a synagogue. Now a divorcee after a failed marriage, she is back in New York at least part time, and I am pleased to see her back in her adopted hometown. Perhaps she will give back some of the love and a few of the good luck charms that the city showered her with during her artistic gestation.

She has also become a film director, which will surely introduce her to new levels of artistic exploration. There is of course no way to tell where her journey will end.

Maybe it's for the best that I never re-connected with Madonna or that I am probably unlikely to ever see her again. This way, I can remember her as she was in her most elemental stage of artistic development. Now that she has moved on to almost unimaginable fame, and I have moved into a quieter life with a family of my own, I would prefer to savor that beautiful era of intersection we shared and perhaps smile from afar.

I wish her all the best.

ABOUT THE AUTHOR

Norris W. Burroughs is a writer and illustrator who was born in Harlem, New York. Burroughs dated Madonna in the fall of 1978, when she had recently arrived in New York from Michigan, several years prior to her amazing success. Madonna's biographers have interviewed Burroughs, and his quotes appear in most accounts of her life, but he has never told his story in his own words. Burroughs feels that it is vital to place Madonna's ascent in the context of the contemporary New York scene.

Burroughs is the Author and Artist of *Voodoo Macbeth*, a graphic novel depicting the events surrounding a 1936 performance of the Shakespeare play that impresario Orson Welles staged and directed. Burroughs father was an actor in said production, playing the part of Hecate, a role that Welles changed to that of a male demonic force.

Burroughs lives with his wife and son in Mill Valley, California.

CPSIA information can be obtained
at www.ICGtesting.com
Printed in the USA
FSHW02n0610081018
52840FS